BREATHE:
101 Contemporary Odes

Edited by

Ryan G. Van Cleave & Chad Prevost

Chattanooga, Tennessee

Copyright © 2009 by Ryan G. Van Cleave and Chad Prevost

All rights reserved

Printed in the United States of America

First Edition

ISBN 10: 0-9815010-1-X
ISBN 13: 978-0-9815010-1-7
LCCN: 2008908169

C&R Press
PO Box 4065
Chattanooga, TN 37405

www.crpress.org

TABLE OF CONTENTS

BREATHE

Editors' Note

Following our instincts for high art, we wanted to assemble an anthology of poems that contained the kind of rich material that keeps you coming back for more, reading and re-reading the way you might listen to a favorite album. At the same time we wanted to pursue our democratic impulses. During this time in which the United States finds itself cloaked in negative forces of all kinds (the war on terror, the failing healthcare system, a sagging economy, corporations parading self-interest seemingly over all other human concerns) we wanted to put together a collection that wasn't against something so much as what it was *for* something positive and life-affirming. Instead of a specific theme which would have possibly narrowed our vision too much, the idea struck for an open-ended form through which such intelligent optimism might shine through.

Our choices were legion, but we thought the antidote to that negativism we sensed might be poems of praise—and that brought us to consider the ode. Again and again, we read that the ode was antiquated or at least seldom used in the 20th century. Like the student told by an instructor not to write a poem about a toothbrush (and who then hurries home to carefully examine his Oral-B with pen and notebook in hand), we accepted the implicit challenge. Our goal was to make the ode a relevant form, or if that seemed too much like we were the Gatekeepers of Poetry, at least help remind people that the ode was a viable mode of expression and meditation as it's been since the days of Pindar, Catullus, and Sappho. For ourselves and others, we wanted to prove that Allen Tate's "Ode on the Confederate Dead" and Wallace Stevens' "The Idea of Order at Key West" weren't the only two good odes written in the past hundred years.

Our own working definition for odes came from Horace, who used the form to construct meditative lyrics on a variety of themes. That seemed simple enough. But the 17th century brought a more formal structure to the form though the work of such poets as John Donne, Ben Jonson, Robert Herrick, and Andrew Marvell. Yet for every metrical marvel such as Shelley's "Ode to the West Wind" (with its fourteen terza rima stanzas) or most of Keats' work, examples of odes with varying line lengths and irregular stanzas are readily found (Samuel Taylor Coleridge and Abraham Cowley, to name just two).

Add in Italy's Chiabrera, France's Ronsard, and Chile's Neruda, and suddenly the ode takes on a highly personal, wide-ranging scope that is impressive. In short, the idea of an ode not as a rigid metrical form but rather as a work of sustained noble sentiment and dignity made it seem flexible enough for nearly any topic. So we decided to test it.

Kenneth Koch and W.S. Merwin have recently published books on odes, taking the rhetorical stance of having poems addressing their subjects directly. We felt, though, that poems can honor and dignify and explore their subjects with an implicit or indirect address. In short, we wanted to open up the form of the ode versus feeling that we were insisting all poems hew to a firm guideline. So, when we put out the call for this anthology that asked contributors to "Feel free to challenge the thematic and stylistic limits of these guidelines (and of the ode form itself)," we wondered if perhaps we *had* gone too far. After all, "elevated style" seemed a given when you're talking about odes, but perhaps in this age of demystification and an anything-goes reality-TV attitude, maybe not. It quickly became clear, though, that the poets sending us work were more in tune with Neruda's *Odas Elementales* and Keats' "Ode to Psyche" than Coldplay's "Ode to My Deodorant" or Adam Sandler's "Ode to My Car." Even when the poem's subject seemed pedestrian, the approach taken was serious, insightful, and worthy. Consider James Arthur's "In Praise of the Semicolon" or Beth Ann Fennelly's "Cow Tipping" for fine examples that support Shelley's view that "Poetry lifts the veil from the hidden beauty of the world, and makes familiar objects be as if they were not familiar." In her commentary on the poem, Katie Chaple adds, "Whenever poets write, they are always writing odes, whether explicitly or implicitly. The very act of writing implies a kind of love or praise if not for the subject matter or the emotions, events, or objects, then for the world in which they exist."

Richard Jackson's "Objects in the Mirror" reminds us of Pindar and the ancient Greek odes with its regularity, its rhythm, and its political/personal concerns. As he says in his commentary, "The ode as a form probably began back with the Greeks, especially Pindar, where it had a more formal, triadic and dialectic structure. Later, Horace, in Rome, loosened the surface format but kept the underlying dialectic structure." Eventually, it became even a looser form, as he notes, "more related to the laments and praises of Neruda and Merwin." Neruda's permeating influence throughout this anthology was one of the unexpected discoveries we witnessed.

While odes such as Elise Paschen's "Sanctuary" and Wendy Vardaman's "St. Catherine of Siena's Day" follow the traditional three-part structure of strophe, antistrophe, and epode, others tend toward the paradoxically-related elegiac tone, such as Gerry LaFemina's "Phenomenology of the Vanishing Horizon," and Vivian Shipley's "An Ode to Virginia Tech, Blacksburg, April 16, 2007." A pleasing mix to be sure.

Sally Ashton's commentary adds that "An ode calls attention to something deserving notice. It seeks to recognize what is worthy." That seems abundantly clear in Robin Behn's ironic "Elegy: Cook County" or the haunting beauty of Sean Brendan-Brown's "A Night So Pure the Love of God Seemed Real." The various paths each author took to achieve compelling poems of praise impressed us and made us want to make the book bigger, but still we held firm to 101, the number that seemed to resonate with us from the start.

From Dick Allen's "Quiet" to Barbara Crooker's "Ode to Chocolate," from Tom Lux's "The Joy-Bringer" to Warren Slesinger's "Wheat," these poems raise up their subjects and turn them in deft hands like a jeweler examining a fine, shimmering diamond. With respect and attention, this gathering of 101 poems by 95 poets showcases some of the most interesting and innovative odes we found in a year of searching. We are pleased with the results, and hope the contributors and readers will be, too.

Christopher Buckley's commentary says: "Most of my poems. . .are looking for the light and hoping to discover and hold some part of transcendence. The poems' projects are to praise and love the world." That's it, we realized. That's what the ode aspires to. That's what every poem aspires to.

Breath. The idea of lifting, taking off, taking *in* life. The air that comes through us to give us voice. The word related to the Latin *vocare* (to call) and to the Greek *inspire* (to be filled with the breath of the gods). It is a title that has developed from the reading of the material for what you will find within. The collective "breath" of this anthology contains a diversity of voice, vision, and style. As Kim Addonizio mentions in her commentary on "God Ode," an ode can be that glimpse of light in an otherwise dark tunnel—a brief sense of glimpse of reason for hope, or expression of beauty or gratitude, or honor of—truly no more or less the size of the subject in praise, and more the perspective of the speaker, the depth of pathos.

Ryan G. Van Cleave & Chad Prevost
September 2008

GOD ODE

Kim Addonizio

Praise having a body to be unhappy in,
suffering the slings and staring unbelieving at the arrows

bristling from your chest as the Indians creep closer.
Praise the oil slick of your loneliness,

the suffocated little shorebirds of your longing.
Here's to the scribbles of alcohol

seeping into the cell walls, the reeling
mitochondria, the deceased brain cells carried out

in coffinettes of sweat. Gratitude, gratitude
to whoever knelt down and shat upon the floor

of the Port-o-Let at the children's playground
where I had to pee last Sunday after pushing my young friend

on the tire swing, after whumping down the curving tube slide
again and again upside down on my back.

Small happiness, followed by nausea—
thank You, thank You! You demented, You disapproving

or possibly AWOL Higher Power.
How high is that anyway? Higher than me

and my grown-up friend doing Ecstasy in the desert,
getting cut up by cactus, floating back to the house

finding water for once more delicious than wine?
Praise You in your aerie, Your maybe-not-there-crag.

Down here on the darkling, fattening plain
we root and toil, and sometimes, mercifully, we spin.

QUIET, QUIET NOW
Dick Allen

As in crossing over the Bourne Bridge
    onto the Cape's curled lobster claw;
as in walking through a redwood forest,
    hands brushing the ferns;
as in the way mist clears from Crater Lake,
    leaving that hallowed blue of snow shadows;
as in the shade of regimental monuments
    off by themselves in Antietam's evening fields;
as in the middle of Kansas
    where all there seems to be is wheat and sky;
as in a glass-bottomed boat
    backing and idling over a coral reef;
as in the trapezoid buttes of Montana,
as in the holy woods of upper Maine,
as in the Storm King Mountain sculptures of David Smith,
as in the ghost towns of Idaho,
as in the Frank Lloyd Wright house where a black piano
    still hangs suspended over narrow stairs;
as in the light that falls into a Hopper painting,
    as on a porch in lower Michigan;
as how a memory of calm
    is like a tall and graceful woman in a summer gown
    standing on the porch, holding the screen door open. . . .

PART 1: ACKNOWLEDGMENT
Ralph Angel

We spin
and we deny it.
We speed through space and
hold our ground. We stand firm.
We sprawl out
in the shadows of cobwebs
and swim to the surface
and toast again the staggering
stars and the planets
and our getting away from it all.
We're nobody's business—
and the truth,
the truth's wooden-clock voice
actually lives here.

When the night sky
for example is spattered with paint
and the forest is reduced
to a few glowing windows
and a curlicue of smoke
above a train,
I was at once inside
our cabin after all, and frankly
sick of friends, though
not the close ones,
of people, maybe,
not you.

Like something in the body
reflecting streets and chance interiors
and yelling Silence,   15
Camera,
your heart, your
family, inappropriately,
your clothes
against my idiocy,
not you.

IN DEFENSE OF THE SEMICOLON

James Arthur

*"No semicolons. Semicolons indicate relationships
that only idiots need defined by punctuation."*
—Richard Hugo

But it's a reassuring logic that rivers freeze
because your hemisphere has rolled away from the sun,
that cities rest because there must be time for resting.
You'd never deny this, or disown your desire
for the certainty of home, for mills and reservoirs
you always return to. I'm thinking of a girl
pinning butterflies through her bangs, the first woman
with whom I spoke of marriage.
She was slight and strange; her brother lived
on another continent, dying there. Years
after our split, she and I met in an open-air restaurant
crowded with chatter and cigarettes. I was still very young,
still afraid of being abandoned at the terminal.
She no longer ate; she had lost teeth and some hair,
she said. There were pale islands of skin
where the butterflies had perched. The waiter came around
to refill our coffee, a phone was ringing, and fifty feet away
streetcars jostled like dusk nudging up against darkness;
even between those two there are gangways:
moveable bridges ship to shore, small therefores.

REMEMBERED LINES ON WAY TO STOCKTON
Sally Ashton

My father owns the cattle on a thousand hills;
they graze among windmills scattered
along the interstate. Beneath a tinfoil moon

it's not quite dark by nine. A silver-sided truck
roars, sucks at my passing car
flashes high beams to let me over.

Bott's dots reflect the headlights,
comets chased by tails along an asphalt skyway.
I have traveled this road all the years of my life,

a journey landscaped with exits never taken
into countryside where mown hay swells blonde
against alfalfa fields already regreening

and words rise from wild grasses
like surprised birds or flock along power lines
draped pole to pole beyond the city limit sign.

I pass the towers for a drawbridge.
It no longer raises over its river,
the only ship a rowboat upended on the bank.

Faded letters on a grain tower
advertise horses for sale. They died
half a century ago.

There is no map for places such as these
that recede in the rear view mirror
and await my return. It is dusk

forever here, with the scent of mowing.
Tonight I drive straight through to Stockton.
My father's mansion has many rooms,

if it were not so I would have told you.
A sudden oasis of farmyard hemmed
by walnut trees. The rising thrum of crickets.

MIDWEST ODE

David Baker

in memoriam William Matthews

You could believe a life so plain it means
calmness in the lives of others, who come
to see it, hold it, buy it piece by piece,
as these good people easing from their van
onto the curb where the big-shoed children
of Charm, Ohio, have lined their baskets
of sweet corn, peaches, green beans, and snap peas.
Each Saturday morning the meeting point
of many worlds is a market in Charm.

You could believe a name so innocent
it is accurate and without one blade
of irony, and green grass everywhere.
Yet, how human a pleasure the silk hairs
when the corn is peeled back, and the moist worm
curls on the point of an ear like a tongue—
how charged the desire of the children who
want to touch it, taste it, turn it over,
until it has twirled away in the dust.

There are black buggies piled high with fruit pies.
There are field things hand-wrought of applewood
and oak, and oiled at the palm of one man.
There are piecework quilts black-striped and maroon

and mute as dusk, and tatting, and snow shawls,
and cozies the colors of prize chickens—
though the corporate farm five miles away
has made its means of poultry production
faster, makes fatter hens, who need no sleep,

so machinery rumbles the nights through.
Still, it is hard to tell who lives with
more placid curiosity than these,
not only the bearded men in mud boots
and city kids tugging on a goat rope,
but really the whole strange market of Charm,
Ohio, where weekly we come, who stare
and smile at each other, to weigh the short
business end of a dollar in our hands.

TO WINTER

David Baker

The poetry of earth
        is never dead.
It flies down, white wind, whipped,
        a swirling snow—
white sound. It's what you hear
        this side of sleep.
One whole side of the house
        seems hurt with it.

And when will you rest who've
        stayed awake for
days, in illness, white woe. . . .
        Even the stripped
pines are an order of
        sleep, the way they
hurt from the shoulder-weight
        of snow, crack, and

fall, their downed limbs blown white.
        Even the wind—.
In the city last week
        you watched the young
beggars, some coins pitched in
        a plate, holding
hands, hold on. Whatever
        they were to each

other, intimate, poor
      relation, a
poor fraud, as passersby
      uttered, hooker
or heroin head, the
      song they offered
was a kind of poetry,
      a kind of sleep

for a soul, if beyond
      measure, fatigued.
And when will deliverance
      be given, in
recompense for our pain . . .
      —and in what coin?
The fallen snow lay humped
      as souls asleep

in doorways, beside curbs,
      as it falls now
and settles, as the blood
      settles in its
own strict poverty. Of
      the white tide
like a vast wind, viral,
      cellular with

snowfall, of a sea blown
      silver rich with
its own fierce destruction,
      Keats feared he gazed
too far through it, as here,
      where every maw
the greater on the less
      feeds evermore.

You watch the days and nights
        in a blinking
eye pass. Ice, wind, snow, white
        wave on wave—the
pine boughs slapped with it—what
        can you offer
but yourself? So the snow
        falls down, like

foliage, and the poet
        puts words away.
Let the poor in spirit
        freeze where they have
gathered at our feet, and
        let the sleeping
begin. The earth knows. Wind—.
        Here follows prose.

ODE TO RED RIDING HOOD
Barry Ballard

There's no way to prove or disprove that we're
really just an experiment sitting
in the middle of someone's checker-clothed
table. And that from time to time, someone
sits in a spindle-legged wooden chair
staring in through the woven coarse knitting
of the border that surrounds us. How lost
(or sometimes, how approachable) our Sun

and its evolving planets must seem, how
our microscopic pin-like orb of blue
atmosphere must seem such an accident
or such a revelation. And there's no
way to prove or especially disprove
if this person possesses an eminent

position in the scheme of things, or if
(by the way of simple things) they might be
as kind and unassuming as anyone's
grandmother. Of course they could be the robed
appearance of the benevolent gift
of free will, disguising the hooded misdeeds
of its own wild creature, a role struck dumb
and afraid to speak, or reveal what it knows.

And the whole thing could have been a prepared
gift, an entire universe of nebula
and newborn stars swinging in the cradle
of a young girl's arm. Venturing the bare
trail of uncertainty in the first forest,
in the first song of a beautiful child.

ELEGY: COOK COUNTY
Robin Behn

Driving through the county
suburban urbane urban ban
my red car beats a path
across quick-plotted plots

    big box sweat shops

my galloping hood ornament
hoping
like the Great Wall and kindness
to be seen from space

    red dot take stock

Underwheel's the underfeel
of farms'
bare ruined shoulders, corn's bumpy hunkered
husks

    dumb stalks knock knock

over which a thousand picturesque invader geese
dip their oily heads
kaching into the motherlode of revved-green
corporate chem-ponds

squawk sop ill got

I come to hunt a woods
I haunted long ago
and that house unbalconied,
unbuxom, unbedecked

skid stocks quadruple locks

but where I did on two wheels and three gears
seek truth is paved and the forests
where I went to weep
are parceled, cutely named

sap slit gist gilt

But I take thee and I dial-in to thy
comingled signals,
thy filament and firmament,
I ride thy girth and grid:

post pasture lost rapture

O Plentious, O Proud, O Fast Asleep
Ingenious Sprawl,
Hog Butcher, Self Butcher,
mall to shining mall.

THE BOOK OF THE DEAD MAN (HIS OLDE ODE)
Marvin Bell

Live as if you were already dead.
–Zen admonition

1. About the Dead Man's Olde Ode

The dead man has been writing the oldster's olde ode.
His oldest ode was the beautiful song, the sound of living at all.
Now ye olde ode is also the news.
Even if there were times when the horizon arced over the planet too acutely to
        reveal the others.
Even if the dead man could not turn enough to see them.
And if the keening of mourners was daily to be pulverized by the sound of motor.
        departing.
Yet the engine of the planet purred, and the wheel sang.
So it was the nature of all and everything that absorbed the dead man.
The world was full of nameless things that words could not keep.
Some wanted the dead man to disown the silence, and he considered it.
He had heard how scary the silence could be.
He knew that an ode to joy had to be thumpingly hearable and make the
        floorboards bounce.
The dead man knew, also, that things end.
His hope was that he be free in the glare of truth to bask in the warm-up to the
        furnace.
And of course to dance.
That he might celebrate before the impact, that he might sing the approach of the
        parasites.

A vase may lie for what we think forever in fragments, but a dead man may not
      be reassembled.
You see that it is well that the dead man has to take a break now and then.
A respite from the olde ode that was, like every pleasure, an escape from time.
The illusions of art have been to the dead man both beautiful and tiring.
The dead man adjusts the piano bench, he resets the reed, he tunes the drum
      and marimba, he turns the pegs at fret's end.
The dead man cannot resist the music of the spheres.

2. More About the Dead Man's Olde Ode

We're back, the self and the other self, the dead man alive and the other one
      looking ahead.
Were you anticipating some hully-gully, some hooey, some hanky-panky?
The dead man has had to forego certain pleasures because of the war.
If you ask which war, take your pick or wait for it.
War is the newsy part of the ode, part of the olde ode and part of the new.
The dead man has been increasingly absorbed by elsewhere and others, he is
      one of them.
The body politic suffered, but the missing arms and legs did not stop him.
Even the cruelest head wounds could not stop the dead man from thinking.
So the dead man apologizes for appearing to celebrate wartime, for he does not.
It was inescapable that pleasure kept on throughout and between the wars, and
      there were many.
The wars were as constant as lawnmowers in the cemeteries.
In time, the dead man no longer pushed the life force into the face of death.
He had become the first patient, he had perfected the wait-and-see.
He had learned, he had looked it up, he had lived through.
The dead man listens for the sounds of involuntary joy.
He hears the treaties shrivel while children laugh in the yard.
He feels the tremor underneath the long lines of laborers and follows the weary
      to the tavern after work.
So long as there can be a few last drops, the dregs, the bottom of the barrel, a
      sip, a taste, a bite, a sniff of the apple, for that long can time-to-come
      retain its welcome.

The dead man's ode was always about the planet and the dance.
It was always about the collapse of empires.
It was always about the silvery cloud edge that winked as it reshaped itself.
He who would last awhile must sprinkle himself widely among all that is not
      himself, you odists listen.

ODE IN SHADES OF GREEN
Eleanor Berry

1.

No white nor red was ever seen
So am'rous as this lovely green.
–Andrew Marvell

Though, in gardens all over the valley, camellias
are thick with white and red
globes of bloom; though the ground beneath each bush
is aproned white and red
with fallen blossoms; though, on a friend's table,
pink and purple tulips flare from a cobalt vase, and,
down street after street, full-crowned dogwoods
glow pink above azalea-brightened borders;

though the rare cardinal lobelia, its intricate
scarlet flower, lured me,
childhood summers, along banks of hidden
woodland brooks, and the radiant white
wild anemone, starring the springtime
forest floor, still quickens my breath; it's green
I would praise, green that quenches thirsty eyes
when it returns after long drought or winter freeze,

green in all the forms of leaf it takes—egg, fan,
wedge, spear, heart, and palm of hand; tender
as petals or fleshy and thick; clasping
the stem or swinging from a stalk; paired, staggered,
or set in a circlet; satin to the touch
or velvet; smooth-edged, scalloped, saw-toothed, lobed,
or cut like lace; single as thumbless mittens or split
like gloves into fingers, feathers into barbs.

Not green, but innumerable greens—golden
green of cottonwoods, newly leafed; deep teal
of Douglas firs, before bright shoots
break from their branch-tips; green lemon
of big-leaf maples' fat, dangling catkins; silvered
green of the pasture grass, mornings when every blade
is coated with dew. No constant hues, but all
continually changing as the season advances—

cottonwoods' amber bud-sap drying away,
dark firs suddenly dotted with vivid points,
emerald maples dulling in summer air,
grassblades' silver vanished in the glare of sun;
the whole palette of the landscape changing until
the green that in spring is foil for blooms
of yellow and purple, white and rose, becomes figure—
woodlots and solitary oaks scattered on tawny slopes.

2.

> *Whatever is fickle, freckled (who knows how?)*
> *With swift, slow; sweet, sour; adazzle, dim . . .*
> *—Gerard Manley Hopkins*

Not green, not even the sheer abundance of greens—
it's greens together, one beside another and all changing,
I would praise. It's greens pricked and splashed
red, white, and every pink and rose between; vernal
marshes lit with yellow spathes of skunk cabbage,
hillsides splotched with yellow broom; long vistas
of green hills receding, stepping into blue, mantled
bronze at sunset, violet in the spreading dusk.

Not green, but the lovely mottle
of red-brown dabs on the trout-lilies'
glistening fish of leaves, surfacing after rain;
not green, but the flicker
of blaze and char, as wind sways the fir-limbs;
not green, but green salad, garnished with nasturtiums,
bouillabaisse, mulligtawny, mingling hot and cool,
stew, compost, potpourri.

It's all that's stippled, checkered, dappled,
I would praise, in all its fragrance and stench.
Not only the delight when land long dormant
returns at last to green, but, equally, the ache
when the blossoms that flounced every bare twig
in the peach orchard with promise
give way to dusty leaves, when the season lurches
unstoppably onward—

MY TATTOO

Erin M. Bertam

Something worth naming as yet without a name.
What's to be said for a bird paused in eternal alight
on forearm, wings spread both away & in embrace?

My paramour. Event horizon. The flesh the first
& quietest defense. Which is not to say insignificant
or any less than other, more hardy variants of armor,

whose weight is implied or otherwise & otherly
borne. Lines sketched, drawn, traced, then memorized,
fingered nights, mornings wildly admired. Once

embossed, the flesh rises in either protest or accord;
what else is to be expected, what response better suited
to dignify such intrusion. Forearm gone all Byzantine

relief, firebird affixed, you rise, a tiny Christ, held
there by layers thin as paper sheaves. Creature born,
creature risen, creature risen again. That Sunday,

under the whirring buzz of mechanized & flourishing
ink, my body held there, willingly, for minutes
at a time. Bird of pyre, bird of soot, bird of cigarette

gone rococo, gone smolder, fixed intaglio, most intimate
intarsia. Wingspan flared feral, silent suspension
between alight & arrival, always impending, always

already there. And its plumage, tenacious, tender
feathers of the neck exposed, an exposé on what it is
to be humble & brazen, &, yes, deservedly holy. Forever

turning in on itself, turning & turning, a face turned
away & quickly back again. As when thick stone wears
the abrasions given it by wind or the beloved palm,

a vestigial translation of its former self. That requisite
turning, effectual in its want, until final swift—
inevitable?—release, sole blue beacon of an eye

amid a whirl of otherwise dynamic, unchanging heat.

ENDURANCE
Michelle Bitting

"...more important than truth."
–Charles Bukowski

You will rise. You will walk from the kitchen
of your demon-scorched dreams,
hear the cool song of larks trilling. Though
the night was a dagger—blood-lusty, twisted—
here is the dawn breaking a sweat
across your pillow, a long yellow massage
for your litany of wounds. Get up. Breathe.
Adorn thy radiant self and consider
the barista on your street, how he brightens
at your face, familiar and wise. Maybe it comes down
to this: a nugget of kindness fished
from misery's stream, a sweet steaming cup
in your hands without asking. And as you wander
the day drinking each new pain,
your tired eyes bent to the boldest print:
mothers wailing—a distant village
where mud has buried a school; more politicians
with their fat pockets, feeble hearts—
now this homeless here
and his one dead eye
begging change from a blanket
he swears is magic, will deliver someday
to the lap of God,
he says, so crazy
you might as well believe him.

ODE TO MEMORY: SELF-PORTRAIT WITH SEVEN FINGERS II
Craig Blais

The first thing I ever saw was a trough. Simple, square,
half hollow, half oval. A market trough.
—Marc Chagall

And the first thing I remember, Chagall, was daylight.
In fact, dust. Particles of dust swirling in the daylight coming through the
    bedroom Window.

The light was still because the dust was dancing in it.

I could still look at it in wonder, too dumb to doubt its charity
Like the promise of air holding the parachute silk high above the children's heads
    in the park,
Or water overflowing, pushing out the ripples, becoming like glass, before it falls.

We are like this, you and I, the trough, and the light and dust inside.

NORTH: 1991

Bruce Bond

In the euphoria that followed
the American air strike
when the New York Exchange soared

over the smoldering cities
and hovered there, a frail spire
aimed at heaven, I was driving

North, like so many who work
in town and live in the canyon.
It was the one road along the icy river

through the narrow tunnel
of my light, the radio cupping
a last match of news in its palm:

I live so close to nowhere.
I've driven this route ten winters,
and never was it so difficult

under the tallest trees,
ice-shagged, splintered,
holding up all of January

as if to give it back.
The highest branches rose
like the antlers of a startled elk.

There was no other way
but up, past the bent girders
over Cold Creek, through the small

fires of snow, layer after layer.
Winter's vault closed without a click.
Higher still where the road turned

into dirt and stone, tapering,
I got out to open the driveway gate
and felt my body grow tight

against the cold. There would be chores,
kindling to gather, a day's weather
in the satellite dish.

But for the time I stopped everything
to stand in the distance
of myself, turning white,

and could hear the thin ecstasy
of saws, the rise and fall,
a crackling in the hard wood.

ENGLISH FLAVORS
Laure-Anne Bosselaar

    I love to lick English the way I licked the hard
round licorice sticks the Belgian nuns gave me for six
good conduct points on Sundays after mass.

    Love it when 'plethora,' 'indolence,' 'damask,'
or my new word: 'lasciviousness,' stain my tongue,
thicken my saliva, sweet as those sticks—black

    and slick with every lick it took to make daggers
out of them: sticky spikes I brandished straight up
to the ebony crucifix in the dorm, with the pride

    of a child more often punished than praised.
'Amuck,' 'awkward,' or 'knuckles,' have jaw-
breaker flavors; there's honey in 'hunter's moon,'

    hot pepper in 'hunk,' and 'mellifluous' has aromas
of almonds and milk. Those tastes of recompense
still bittersweet today as I roll, bend and shape

    English in my mouth, repeating its syllables
like acts of contrition, then sticking out my new tongue—
flavored and sharp—to the ambiguities of meaning.

MILES DAVIS PLAYS TRUMPET AT THE FUNERAL OF MALCOLM X

Earl Sherman Braggs

I could begin by tell you
he rode two horses at once
without falling off only to fall
between the legs of the Nation of Islam.

I could tell you that this is Harlem 1965
and Malcolm is still standing there
next to that dying room window
peeping out through a rifle and a scope,
but I won't.

What I will tell you is this: today is Sunday.
Sunday is movie day at the Folsom County Prison.
We are watching a John Wayne picture show
in slow motion black and white, 16 mm.
Outside it's raining crows.

Inside this place is a storm brewing in a percolating pot,
so death is no stranger when he comes
quiet as a whisper in a movie-dark room
full of men. "Malcolm X is dead."

I cannot describe the smell of fear
in a cup of hot coffee too black to drink,

spilling onto my lap, spilling onto the front page
of every newspaper locked in boxes on every street corner.
Here's a dime for 10 pages of lies.

I know it as it was.
"He was standing and he fell,
he fell and he died." That's all.
Now he is no more than a photograph
on the back of an Alex Haley comic book Superman.

Look at me. I am a comic. Laugh.
It's a funny thing how things happen
just like in the movies. Just like Errol Flynn.
Just like Tyrone.

Just like me. I've been here 3 years, 17 days
and 9 hours. Sometimes at night
I turn out the light and dream backwards
betweens these bars and stripes and stars,
always movie stars.

But this ain't no movie house popcorn picture show
sticking to the floor. It's blood
that makes a wedding rose red enough
to decorate the dead.

Outside the rain has stopped,
but the crows are gone.
They are hovering over the kill.
The movie is over and yes
John Wayne got the girl.

Drinking cold coffee and smoking my cigarettes
down to the very end, I'm the only one left
sitting here in the middle of a sold-out show,

staring at Minister Malcolm laid out
in the stately manner of royalty.

A trumpet begins to blow, softly at first then slow.
I turn to see the image of a man
leaning back into a corner blacker than he is.
Miles is blowing back the pages of "Someday
my Prince will come."

A NIGHT SO PURE THE LOVE OF GOD SEEMED REAL

Sean Brendan-Brown

I haven't my glasses on, it's all Monet-vision
under the belling of a horned owl from a column
of shadow, a fretwork of wind in the unpruned
mimosa's barely fragrant diluted-blood colored
flowers, the beetle-scarred linden, scent syrupy,
starkly silver in moonlight. The crash I awoke to
may be nothing, a dog at garbage, blown-over
deck chair; I am in awe of this gorgeous night,
so grateful to be alive I'll face any danger, brew
the ax-murderer lurking downstairs tea and say

take this, it's French breakfast, my favorite. I'd
lead him from room to room, point out the silver
spoon's anthracite patina; the ancient Dell &
chugging Epson, four dollars three quarters two dimes
by half a Papa John's Hawaiian; a snarl of keys to
forgotten doors & the nine-year-old Nissan: cat & me,
leave us alone—I'll forfeit all but our lives—for our
lives I'll fight. The saint with unkindly eyes watches:
it's an old painting of Jerome, not worth anything,
just old. Shrubs stir, vines hiss, the breeze, laden

with nicotiana, scatters ash from my cigarette.
The cedars slant east, twisted that direction before my
birth; I heave the window up another inch, can't get
enough of shady blooms, moon clouded yet enough
light that yellowing serviceberry & callery pear
bubble like sulfur—the mystery and music
insects make with desperate strength is a hymn—
song for the highland heifer and lowland
loon, for shining clusters the moon creates
breaking out over ordinary junk.

SYCAMORE CANYON NOCTURNE

Christopher Buckley

But home is the form of the dream, & not the dream.
—Larry Levis

Home again in dreams, I'm walking that foothill road
as the last morning star slips away over canyon walls—
red-gold riprap of creek rock, ferns splayed in the blue
shade of oaks, the high yellow sycamores, oat straw catching
sun at my feet. Wind-switch, then the chalk-thick stillness
saying angels, who come down here to dip their wings
and give the water its color.
                    Yet even when I'm allowed back
along the weedy path of sleep to this green and singing space,
I know someday air will be set between my shoulder blades
and arms and all my bones, and, little more than clouds,
the clouds will be my final lesson until I'm taken off
into some clearer imagining . . . .
                    In exile, it is hard to love God.
What then, must I renounce? The Psalter of evergreens
ringing along Sheffield Drive? The loquat and acacia
burning through ocean fog? Can I speak of love
almost a life ago, syllables repeating the skin's sweet salts
and oils like lemon blossoms riding the August heat?
I love the life slowly taken from me, so obviously spun out
flower-like, and for my own use, it seems, against some future
sky—the world, just a small glory of dust above a field
one autumn afternoon—the resinous pines and a back road
full of birds inside you.

            What more could wishes be,
who would live there again, sent back among the breathing
acanthus to lift unconsciously with morning and with mist?
I would.
            Moonlight or dreamlight, this is the world, giving
and taking away with the same unseen hand, desires winding
around the soul like fleshy rings on a tree. Where this canyon
levels out, I'd eat the wild sun-red plums, the sweet light
of the juice carrying through me my only hymn.

I know God, old flame wearing through the damp sponge
of the heart, that candle I cannot put out, coming back
each time it seems extinguished. And so I must bless everything,
take anything given me—these words, their polish or pity,
the absences they bear like winter trees ascending
the ridge, so many angels starving in the early dusk,
and then the dark, and the broken order of prayer . . . .

I know you are listening. Like the sky. And the birds
going over, aren't they always full of light? But to shine
like these trees again, that air hovering on the canyon walls—
sometimes, all I want to be is the dreaming world.

DISPATCH FROM THE GARDEN AT 57

Christopher Buckley

I love the red-winged blackbirds taking their places on the phone lines for the falling light. And the squads of crows rowing home out of the far blue after a day in the broccoli and artichoke fields—I love them and all that high, unheard music, the intuitive cantatas slip-streaming along up there. If I look back past the canyons sunk off shore, past the plates of shale cantilevered against the sky, even past the two royal palms reaching up from this mesa—rustling, tilting back and forth with their invisible knowledge—what deeper realizations really await me?

So I praise the purple bottlebrush, my bed of double delight roses, the thick, rouged cheek of late afternoon. I love each deep breath I take here, away from everything, love looking up along side the pomegranates and pittosporum, the ornamental plum—one more thing still breathing. I love the yellow grass of January I don't have to mow, and the self-sufficient sandstone hills, life still at every turn as the bronzed atmosphere mists down.

The sky glazes over with opalescent clouds, and my cat, Cecil B., charges across the yard after shadows and the come-ons of gusts among the weeds. I fan my fingers like the sheet music of the light, I think a little about a poem escaping on the air. I pick up my dialogue with the hard-skinned lemon tree and do not worry about the wind, the separation of clouds and bones, the smoke drifting away like my aspirations . . . .

I'm lighting up my last Cubano,—a Romeo y Julieta my student gave me, hand delivered by his father from the island—I'm celebrating with an Italian bar glass full of double-wood single malt, a gift from my old friend, a Chicano who lives up the street—somehow, even back of beyond in Lompoc, there's an almost international atmosphere today.

But it's cold for California. The hummingbirds have gone south, far, I'm sure, past Santa Barbara where no one can now afford to live. I throw on my gray-blue Rugby shirt and thus match the winter light wearing thin over the west, shining like the knees on my good pair of slacks. It's a Ralph Lauren Polo, $2.95 at the Salvation Army Thrift—Rugby and Polo, two sports I've just recently given up. But the shirt fits, and so I wear it—pride and irony dispersed in equal parts when you can afford not to ask, How Much?

You hit plateaus in life, you think you know things—but at any level, there's been no salvation in sight. And, given a liberal arts education, when I think of how I might improve my station in life, Aristotle comes to mind—how, puzzled by the inexplicable current off the coast of Boeotia, he jumped into the swirling water for enlightenment; or Empedocles, who, nearing death and wanting to be thought a god, vanished into thin air by throwing himself into the fires of Mt. Etna. There are, however, some things self-defeating with regard to career.

Like Cecil, I've adjusted to the friendly confines of Lompoc. He loves the inexpensive brand of Chicken Feast and at 16+ pounds could care less about irony. When he's cleaned his plate, he just wants out the front for a punch-up with whoever has it coming, a pursuit which, more often than not, damages advancement—I let a thought about work and department politics dissipate. I'd give him a dram of my single malt if it would calm him—it works for me in the twilight these days. For now, he's content on the chaise longue, keeping me company on my birthday. My wife is at Yoga class, and I again assume the position, Sea Lion at Rest. I have salmon filet and yellow squash for dinner, but no cake, not a crumb of carbohydrate—on this diet over a year now, everything I try works as well as prayer . . . .

57 today. Firing up this puro and watching the smoke drift heavenward, the starry flow chart unfurl, still unreadable.

Today, it's inconsequential that I am older by a year than yesterday—always, there are the same number of bricks to hoist up hill. Still, no matter what God's left unfinished, I've done my work. So I'll leave everything to the sea that, like a bill collector, is never far from my door—the dark sea, where today, alone or not, I've decided I will be happy, drifting in the small boat of my heart.

RAIN

Elena Karina Byrne

It all began in hunger.

Once there were two brothers. They were twins, but their nine mouths
were all they had in common.

Beget-began with the rain in velvet swags,
white doves that flew from the pie,
an opened umbrella

of spun sugar, rosebud colored, synonym for the time
it takes to hold back tears.
The face & face, vivid, each, the liqueur-glass of it poured
over the floating photograph.

Felt it, you have, in your chest, pour down the ribs, repeating
each grief. It falls to the Earth, all in longing,
respires from plants, falls to join itself, relief rain, orographic,
meeting mountains from the sea to what rain shadow region reasons there,
blown & blown

in oral repetition, round in bubble, wind & cloud overhead,

silvering celestial dew,
this muslin horizon coming toward you

with wool-gatherers, asking, asking until your hair is soaked, shirt, now
second skin... Someone, who swims in you,

is undoing the rain's waistcoat around the house,
is cooking the books of misfortune
for you, lemon, oil and water, bride of the wind to raise
                              the roof, revere, rolling the deep gut-wheel
under linden tree, or sacred guango
carrying its cicadas in their machine-shearing song, their sound
like rain falling into its future thirst,

                    so very leeward, windward on your side, saturated,

like the hung laundry there,
bringing in dog of gusts and gale cats, the down-pouring
sorrowful sentence of a single day,
                    sprung harbinger of many more...

YOU AND SHE WANT TO DRIVE ALL NIGHT—

Katie Chaple

as though it were like flipping
through a magazine, a catalogue
picking the perfect galvanized tub or gardening gloves
or backdoor mat. Your bodies, side by side,
pitch together down some dark patch,
radio light glowing your fingers green
as you tune to the next song singing
you along highway, the soft peach
of luck hanging before you. Your tongues turn foreign
in the dark, syllables strange and disjointed, but translated
as the seeds of fields transform to towns, then back
into land looking like fathoms
at some soft hour. Shocks and struts
buoyant, you are both vigilant to each curl
of the road because all squeaks with possibility.
You will both decide where to land—no
destination, just hoping to be lost
and found in the same breath. Coiling the night
in, orchards bloom as you approach
sunrise, and you heap your senses—your faces flaming,
your eyes burn. And your hearts?
                    Your hearts, open mouths.

TO SOLDIER

Maxine Chernoff

"My traditional Christ-image was somehow inadequate."
–CG Jung

Grateful for bread
grateful for toast
grateful for deployment
to a bridge under a freeway

Under the sway of winter
wars command the world
satellites in space
and praise is underdone

Pleasant as an ache
remembered for its lie
first it was a place
now it's come to this

Underneath the sky
glaciers sink and fall
a thousand and more men
die before they know

Grateful for wars
generals make their case
we need this you know
to comfort and seduce

So they die for you
with summer in the air
breathless with belief
we understand your loss

Grateful for lambs
whitewashed on snow
grateful for delusions
and a thousand flying geese

FORECAST

Kelly Cherry

The bombs are not falling yet—
Only snow, wet snow, thick snow. Storybook snow.
Yet like most of us, I keep waiting for the bombs.
We know that one day the weatherman will say,
Good morning, America! Dress warmly.
Stay indoors if you can. Try not to drive.
And now for the outlook. Observe
Our wonderful satellite photograph:
In this area, we expect a high-pressure area
Of MX missiles, and over here, to this side
Of the Rockies, something is brewing,
Something radioactive. But cheer up.
This is only the outlook. Weather is wonderful;
It can always change. For today,
Your typical air masses are cold but stable,
And the SAC umbrella remains furled
In the closet of its silos, underground bases,
And twenty-four-hour sky-watches. Today
We have snow, wet snow, thick snow. Storybook snow.
Today we are going to live happily ever after.

IN THE WORKSHOP AFTER I READ MY POEM ALOUD

Don Colburn

All at once everyone in the room says
nothing. They continue doing this and I begin to know
it is not because they are dumb. Finally

the guy from the Bay Area who wears his chapbook
on his sleeve says he likes the poem a lot
but can't really say why and silence

starts all over until someone says she only has
a couple of teeny suggestions such as taking out
the first three stanzas along with

all modifiers except "slippery" and "delicious"
in the remaining four lines. A guy who
hasn't said a word in three days says

he too likes the poem but wonders why
it was written and since I don't know either
and don't even know if I should

I'm grateful there's a rule
I can't say anything now. Somebody
I think it's the shrink from Seattle

says the emotion is not earned and I wonder
when is it ever. The woman on my left
who just had a prose poem in *Green Thumbs & Geoducks*

says the opening stanza is unbelievable
and vindication comes for a sweet moment
until I realize she means unbelievable.

But I have my defenders too and the M.F.A. from Iowa
the one who thinks the you is an I
and the they a we and the then a now

wants to praise the way the essential nihilism
of the poem's occasion serves to undermine
the formality of its diction. Just like your comment

I say to myself. Another admires the zenlike polarity
of the final image despite the mildly bathetic
symbolism of sheep droppings and he loves how

the three clichés in the penultimate stanza
are rescued by the brazen self-exploiting risk.
The teacher asks what about the last line

and the guy with the chapbook volunteers it suits
the poem's unambitious purpose though he has to admit
it could have been worded somewhat differently.

ODE TO CHOCOLATE
Barbara Crooker

I hate milk chocolate, don't want clouds
of cream diluting the dark night sky,
don't want pralines or raisins, rubble
in this smooth plateau. I like my coffee
black, my beer from Germany, wine
from Burgundy, the darker, the better.
I like my heroes complicated and brooding,
James Dean in oiled leather, leaning
on a motorcycle. You know the color.

Oh, chocolate! From the spice bazaars
of Africa, hulled in mills, beaten,
pressed in bars. The cold slab of a cave's
interior, when all the stars
have gone to sleep.

Chocolate strolls up to the microphone
and plays jazz at midnight, the low slow
notes of a bass clarinet. Chocolate saunters
down the runway, slouches in quaint
boutiques; its style is je ne sais quois.
Chocolate stays up late and gambles,
likes roulette. Always bets
on the noir.

ODE TO THE REEL MOWER
Jim Daniels

When you stop pushing
it stops exactly there
absorbing the grace
of cut-grass silence.

*

It always starts. It never runs
out of gas. It does not
shoot your eye out
with a rock or glass shard.

*

It runs on dew and pollen
and sweat. It has never
woken one sleeping person.
It is never new and improved.

*

Grass falls gentle
onto itself like pages
of a favorite book.

*

If the blades need sharpening
a 150-year-old man with a large stone
in a damp basement will send up
faint sparks, accept no payment.

*

At night it trims
the moon's beard.

STARFISH

Chad Davidson

Such brilliant boredom under the sun.
How they carve shadows in the moon-

dust of the ocean floor, each arm
radiant, excruciating

to the thousand hungry mouths
they tease: small wonder

we try to thank them. Lucky ones
in tanks in low-lit city aquariums,

or those desiccated on the shore—
in time we find these stars

more precious than what we count on.
Orbiting in glass skies

foreign to their silences, we puzzle
over their power to regenerate,

how the stories their bodies make
replay. In Hollywood,

we walk their silhouettes, unaware
how they fell there. Seeing stars

over the infant—they swing
from cribposts in primordial dark.

Odd angels thrown into a fire
of coastlines crowned with bodies,

and which of us could rip their wings
in greed, demystify them,

break our promise to continue
with these myths we made,

sunk in constellations
we guide our lives by?

ODE TO AN OPHTHALMOLOGIST
Todd Davis

The doctor asks me to roll my eye toward the ceiling
so she can insert the small brace that will keep my lids
open during the procedure. For weeks the bump
has festered beneath my right eye—first a scab, then
ooze of pus, then another scab. The bright orange
antibiotic has not worked, nor the steroidal drops
that burned the eye, reduced the swelling, yet finally
could not conclude anything. Now this incision—
the only recourse to my sons' averted gazes, my wife's
pitying stare. Because I no longer look as intently
in the mirror as I did at fifteen—every girl a possible
dance partner, a potential kiss—I forget when others
see me that my eye droops, listless and lethargic.
I'm glad I feel nothing as the doctor scrapes clean
the wound she has made. She tells me the infection
looks like clear cottage cheese, reminds me to use
warm compresses, that the eye may still close shut
and again make a not so benign bump. What will
I take from this? A scar. The memory of the nurse
who became sick at the sight and had to leave.
How my eye opened again to the world; how it seemed
nothing had changed.

ON THE BUS TO PITTSBURGH

Carl Dennis

Ordinarily, I wouldn't bother a stranger
I met on the bus with my plan
For saving the country. But you
Seem like a person ready to listen.
I take those brochures you've been studying
About walks through Wales and Scotland
To mean you're eager to leave this country
Whenever you can, that you've concluded,
As I once did, that change is impossible
Here where the people seem to enjoy believing
The lies their leaders enjoy concocting.
But may I suggest you're ignoring
Evidence like our jury system
Whose basic reliability proves we still care,
Now and then, about justice?
That's where my plan comes in,
Which begins with putting our voting machines
In storage an choosing our leaders
As we do our juries, by lottery.

Are you with me so far, or does your silence
Mean you don't believe I'm a practical person?
Try suspending your doubts for a while
And asking yourself how you might feel

If at the next stop an official got on
To announce that we aren't headed to Pittsburgh
As scheduled, that the luck of the lottery
Has chosen our group for Washington.
Of course, we'd cry out in protest
At the thought of the wounds
That four years away from home
Would inflict on our schedules.
But wouldn't our outrage be evidence
We were free of the lust for power
That now contaminates most contenders?

I hope I'm right in supposing your looking around
Doesn't mean you're thinking of changing seats,
Just that you're wondering, as I am,
If our fellow riders show any obvious sign
Of potential for public service. What's your opinion
Of that thin young woman four rows ahead
Adjusting her makeup in her compact mirror
As if to charm he way through the world?
Do you think she can scold a Cabinet
Into consensus? The odds she'll try
Don't seem to me any worse than the odds
Those noisy poker players behind us
Will decide it's time to forgo bluffing and posturing.
As for the old woman behind the driver,
Don't you agree that her dowdy,
Flowery hat might be a sign of a confident
Disregard for the crowd's opinion
That could offer a new regime some integrity?

In a minute I'll let you get back to your reading,
I promise. The brochure with the cover photo
Of Hadrian's Wall looks interesting. Also the one
Showing a tent pitched by a dark-age ruin.

But if ruins are what attract you,
You don't have to go abroad.
Plenty of chances here for a busload
Of leaders-to-be to feel like travelers
Musing among the stumps of toppled columns
Strewing a Forum, travelers with the job
Of deciding which temples to rebuild first thing.

For me, of course, it all goes back to the question
Which gods might be willing to accept our lottery
As a call for help. And then the question what steps
Would we like them to sponsor first
So our path leads us to voting booths
Lit better than the booths we're used to,
Those closet caves, those dungeons.

TO A (BUICK) SKYLARK

Travis Wayne Denton

Teach me half the gladness
That thy brain must know,
Such harmonious madness
From my lips would flow
The world should listen then,
as I am listening now!
—Percy Bysshe Shelley

Crooning in the driveway with your thirty-five year old grin,
idling over the miles you've driven to make it to my door,
do you remember driving I-40 all night, hammer down,
ghost towns clicking off the map like daisy petals fall in spring rain,
engine humming, drinking gasoline like sailors slam shots of gin?
Do you often think of those nights at some frosty Lover's Lane,
windows fogged as you rocked on your axles? Did you wish then,
you could stay until morning, waiting for the sun to palm the rusty sandstone
scattered around you? How many times did you wish
you could set pen to page and send postcards home,
snapshots recording a purple sun dipping behind the Sandias,
water rushing through the hot springs at Jemez,
or simply how the broken white lines urged you on another mile,
a tether pulling you to Vegas, or on to L. A.
or back South, your home—dear God, if only there was something
you left there, something to get back or reconcile?
And when you saw, as you must have, buzzards spiraling
down just off the roadside, did they remind you, as they often do me,
of dying—did you imagine your golden skin flaking in the sun,

or those tired mornings to come when you just can't move an inch,
only groan and sputter—those days like today when breath
is frozen smoke with someone like me cheering you on,
sitting with you, an aged wreck refusing consolation
like a bad child, overtired, wanting nothing more than to be left alone.

PUERTO NUEVO
David Dominguez

Dazed, but with the keys to our new house in my pocket,
        my wife and I flee the San Joaquin Valley
                and drive to Baja where the sea

will soothe our rattled hearts as we lean over our cabin's balcony
        and inhale the mist coming off the rocks where the waves land.
                I've needed this trip for months,

for building a house was a bigger task than I could have expected,
        and it showed: I forgot haircut appointments,
                ran stop signs, and enjoyed, at the mini mart,

too many hot dogs and Big Gulps
        while catching my breath between
                the real estate agent, the bank, and the builder.

So now I've gained weight in the wake of selecting
                floor plans, ceiling heights, elevations, and fixtures—
                        all of which fried my nerves.

Today, the keys are in my pocket, but today, I'm also broke,
        which is why my wife said one Hail Mary over a votive candle
                before we left for Mexico;

perhaps I should call it penance since this morning I cleaned out
        the savings to take this trip—a sin I pray
                doesn't leave us short and in a squeeze....

When I was twenty-one years old, I was more broke than I am now,
    but I owned a red truck and the selected poems of
        William Carlos Williams that I'd read during dinner.

For weeks, I survived on bread and a large can of jalapeños
    that I worked over even after the inside
        began to rust and smelled

too ripe for even a student studying literature.
    I longed for nothing more than my truck bed
        and a sky filled with stars that I knew

held more poems than I would ever write.
    The sky above of the valley now usually holds nothing
        but light pollution bouncing off dust

let alone a moment of duende riding like a sword between
    the shoulders of Taurus—but in Puerto Nuevo today,
        I've found again my wife's hip,

and I've put my hand there as we browse through road-side shops
    because she wants, for storing tequila, a decanter
        the color of the house Diego built Frida,

a knick-knack that we can't afford; still, my hand is
    on her hip when we enter Mariscos del Mar, a restaurant
        with windows that look upon the sea,

and it's there when we sit down and order lobster, beans, rice, and beer—
    there as if I'm marking in a book a poem that I know
        I'll need to read over and over

the way my heart needs the sea, the way my mind needs thoughts
    as quiet as butter melting in a tortilla
        fresh off a flame.

VIEW OF THE PALISADES (1967)

William Doreski

John George Brown placed a steamboat,
a side-wheeler with two tall flagstaffs,
smack in the middle of his canvas.

To the right, another side-wheeler,
a couple of tugboats, and several
pointed sailboats. To the left,
a landing place, a wooden pier,
boathouses, and up the slope
a clutch of verandahed houses.

Under a lint-colored sky
the big shrug of the Palisades
in autumn rust is convincing,
the finely crumpled texture
of the Hudson palpable as flesh.

The overall effect is warm
enough to convince the viewer
that the American nineteenth
century was a comforting place,
despite the Robber Barons,

replete with cheery umber vistas,
coppery-sienna rivers,
steamboats that unlike the one
that killed Louisa Hawthorne
never exploded.
                Henry James
knew better than the painters
how bottomless the Hudson was;

but I'd like to believe Mr. Brown
that on this day two years after
the assassination of Lincoln
and the close of the Civil War
America had so completely healed

that in this leathery autumn light
anyone might imagine himself
about to walk upon water.

ODE TO THE FERRIS WHEEL, ON ITS 99th BIRTHDAY

Denise Duhamel

June 1992

Oh, Mr. Ferris, what an invention!
Your diagrams and blueprints, your wild imaginings
finally turning, slow and high that initial time—
the toast of the fair, rising over the rest
of flat Chicago. I feel like one of the first to ride
this night of my birthday, a century later
in another city, another state. The summer
moon is rosy pink and maybe it's the climbing
and falling like sex that makes the man
who stands in front of my lover and I in the long line
boast he's taken the same girl on this ride
for twenty-six years in a row. His wife blushes,
half of her coy, the other half embarrassed
that her husband's so loud. I will be married
in a couple of months, and in my mind
my ring twirls like Mr. Ferris's first initials:
W. G. W. Letters coming back
to eclipse themselves. Ford Madox Ford.
William Carlos Williams. The palindrome
of my birth date and age: 13 and 31.
My lover and I will kiss, sure
we are blessed, every time
we go over the top crest.
The luck of the circle and the sun.

ALABANZA:
IN PRAISE OF LOCAL 100
Martín Espada

*for the 43 members of Hotel Employees and Restaurant Employees
Local 100, working at the Windows on the World restaurant, who
lost their lives in the attack on the World Trade Center*

Alabanza. Praise the cook with a shaven head
and a tattoo on his shoulder that said *Oye,*
a blue-eyed Puerto Rican with people from Fajardo,
the harbor of pirates centuries ago.
Praise the lighthouse in Fajardo, candle
glimmering white to worship the dark saint of the sea.
Alabanza. Praise the cook's yellow Pirates cap
worn in the name of Roberto Clemente, his plane
that flamed into the ocean loaded with cans for Nicaragua,
for all the mouths chewing the ash of earthquakes.
Alabanza. Praise the kitchen radio, dial clicked
even before the dial on the oven, so that music and Spanish
rose before bread. Praise the bread. *Alabanza.*

Praise Manhattan from a hundred and seven flights up,
like Atlantis glimpsed through the windows of an ancient aquarium.
Praise the great windows where immigrants from the kitchen
could squint and almost see their world, hear the chant of nations:
*Ecuador, México, Republica Dominicana,
Haiti, Yemen, Ghana, Bangladesh.*
Alabanza. Praise the kitchen in the morning,
where the gas burned blue on every stove

and exhaust fans fired their diminutive propellers,
hands cracked eggs with quick thumbs
or sliced open cartons to build an altar of cans.
Alabanza. Praise the busboy's music, the chime-chime
of his dishes and silverware in the tub.
Alabanza. Praise the dish-dog, the dishwasher
who worked that morning because another dishwasher
could not stop coughing, or because he needed overtime
to pile the sacks of rice and beans for a family
floating away on some Caribbean island plagued by frogs.

Alabanza. Praise the waitress who heard the radio in the kitchen
and sang to herself about a man gone. *Alabanza.*

After the thunder wilder than thunder,
after the shudder deep in the glass of the great windows,
after the radio stopped singing like a tree full of terrified frogs,
after night burst the dam of day and flooded the kitchen,
for a time the stoves glowed in darkness like the lighthouse in Fajardo,
like a cook's soul. Soul I say, even if the dead cannot tell us
about the bristles of God's beard because God has no face,
soul I say, to name the smoke-beings flung in constellations
across the night sky of this city and cities to come.
Alabanza I say, even if God has no face.

Alabanza. When the war began, from Manhattan and Kabul
two constellations of smoke rose and drifted to each other,
mingling in icy air, and one said with an Afghan tongue:
Teach me to dance. We have no music here.
And the other said with a Spanish tongue:
I will teach you. Music is all we have.

ODE TO YOUR EARRINGS
Martín Espada

for Katherine

There are parrots of the Amazon peeking from your hair.

On your earlobes twin Taíno goddesses of the river
squat, their eyes in slits, and dream
the cloud of underwater birth.
Here two Zuni dancers bend and breathe
into their flutes;
here float the smallest leaves and pine cones
from Thoreau's sanctuary,
woven on the loom of trees.

Your ears must be the shoreline
of an ocean after the hurricane:
the seahorses of Thailand curl their tails,
brushing your neck;
purple wooden fish flit past,
hiding in the shade of your hand
when you stroke your hair;
the fish of clay hide, too, shunned by the others
because their skin is fired earth;
and the silver dolphins somersault
in an arc forged like a sickle.

Gold coins pressed from fingers to ears
in the mirror bring a flash
of fingers shoveling the mines.

You keep the plastic pearl earrings
of my grandmother so your hands will know
the Bronx, coffee in a sock on the stove,
the sewing machine's stinger.

One earring lost: dried violets widowed,
turquoise stone in a shield left to tarnish,
peacock feathers painted blue with yellow eyes
still searching for a mate, solitary amethyst,
diminutive lion of wood hunting alone.

But in your ears
you hear the Zuni flute, the branches
shuttling their loom, the dolphin chatter,
a prayer at the wake of the gold miner.
You nod at my grandmother's tranquilidad
de Puerto Rico, serene as the sewing machine at rest.
The goddesses and birds chant in your hair
the recipe for the creation of planets.

Then you stir me from my sleep,
and at night you tell me what you hear.

WITH AND WITHOUT
Richard Fein

Faith without reason pilots heaven-falling planes into tall buildings
and shakes boulders off mountains quaking with artillery shells.
Faith without reason is the conscience of the holier slaughtering the thou
and the false god's reward for offerings of burnt flesh.
Faith without reason stokes fiery hordes with the courage of charging lemmings
and is the inventor of the rack and thumbscrew.
Faith without reason garbles the sermons of Moses, Mohammad, and Jesus
and disowns loving daughters and sons for their slightest sins.
Faith without reason decrees, "And thus it is written"
and no reciter of such scripture dare change even one word.

Reason without faith cheers both goosestepping invaders
and subsequent liberators just as loudly.
Reason without faith sells vials of plague in backrooms
for a handsome up-front profit.
Reason without faith is a chess grandmaster
making pawns, knights, bishops, castles, and even queens
gambits to checkmate kings.
Reason without faith turns thumbs down on gladiators
if it pleases the paying audience.
Reason without faith gives a fat man sweet dreams among the starving
and a well-equipped lifeboat among the drowning.
Reason without faith is a cool sexy swinger with AIDS and without a condom,
and whose clever answers make a liar out of a polygraph.
Reason without faith is the jaded priest's filibuster at the pulpit.

And without faith and without reason the two towers that hold up the sky
collapse like some weary Atlas's arms.
But with reason and with faith the ramrod towers are rebuilt
just shy of the ziggurat of Babel,
but high enough so the gleaming glass reflects sunlight on all below.

COW TIPPING

Beth Ann Fennelly

I think I did it three, four times, at least—sneak out, ride
with some boys in a truck to a farm, hop the fence with our flashlights
and Coors while the small frogs fled the machetes of our feet,
crash through grass to where the Holsteins clustered, slumbered,
grass-breathed, milk-eyed, high as my shoulder, weighing a ton
and worth a grand: they'd topple with a single, bracing shove.

The yoke of their shoulders thundered the ground
and we'd feel it through our feet as we ran, whooping,
me nearly wetting my pants with adrenaline and fear—
those cows could toss me like a sack of trash, snap my bones
like balsa, though mostly what they did was roll to their stomachs,
shake their stupid heads, unfold their forelegs, heave-ho to their feet.

By then we'd be racing home, taking curves so fast
we'd slam against the doorframe, turn up the Springsteen,
me on some guy's knees, dew-slick, grass-etched—
another pair of white Keds ruined—check me out, puffing Kurt's
menthol Marlboro although I didn't smoke. Cough cough.
I could end this by saying how I ran with the boys and the bulls

and no one ever harmed me. I was a virgin then, stayed that way
for years, though I wore Victoria's Secret beneath my uniform skirt.
And no one ever harmed me. But I'm lifting off in a half-empty plane

which clears a field of cows, the meek, long-suffering cows,
and from this heightened window I can't understand
why I can't understand why whole countries hate our country.

Because of our bemused affection for our youthful cruelties.
Because the smug post-prandial of nostalgia coats the tongue.
Somehow, despite the planes clearing fields of cows and flying
into buildings full of red-blooded Americans, it's still so hard
to accept that people who've never seen me would like to see me
dead, and you as well. Our fat babies. Our spoiled dogs.

And I, a girl at thirty-two, who likes to think she was a rebel, who lifts
like a crystal this tender recollection every few years to the bright window
of her consciousness, or lobs it into a party for a laugh—Cow tipping?
I've done that—who brags (isn't it a brag?) that no harm
ever came to her—what would they make of me, the terrorists
and terrified? Wouldn't they agree I've got it coming?

REQUIEM FOR THE SINKING CITY

Carmen Firan

it takes naiveté to believe the tales
of the old knife thrower
the blues dancer on the alligator's back
from which he'll fashion evening bags
and binding for books
written in the language of dream
madmen who with sound and fury besiege
the streets of the Vieux Carré

shutters from colonial houses float downriver
coffins wrapped in Mardi Gras beads
carry the last pharaohs of the food-can pyramids

the blind saxophonist sets his shoes to dry in a voodoo-shop window
he snaps his soul down as if dealing
the fool from whom the archangel tattooed with blue hearts
bets against crew-cut angels
witches fly on a single wing aborting babies
little clay devils who cavort among dancers' feet

it takes naiveté to believe that this century will ever wake up
from its bloody hangover of the senses
the world's placenta bubbles muddy waters

death swims on her back
pulling behind her the last streetcar

SWEETGUM COUNTRY
Ann Fisher-Wirth

Billy shows us his arm, burned by the sun
where pesticides sensitized his skin
those years of his childhood, playing
in Delta cotton fields. A charred,
hand-sized lozenge marks the tender crease
inside his elbow. Alex holds up her chart
that shows the sickness and death
in her mother's family, from cancer
in Cancer Alley. She has made red circles
for "fought," green crosses for "died,"
she has put stars around her name,
my pretty dark-haired student.
They come to class, my sixteen freshmen,
and no matter what their topics,
they all say, "I never knew this..."

Fords and Chevies that will barely crank
one more time are parked in the reeds
and slick red mud. Early evening sun
pours down on the cypresses and sweetgum,
the Tallahatchie swamp at the edge
of Marshall County. Turtles poke their heads up.
Cottonmouths zipper through black water
or stretch out long and bask on the abandoned

railroad bridge. Men and women of all ages
beguile the hours after work,
the idle hours, with soft talk or silence,
with bamboo poles and battered coolers.
They could use the food.
They fish for buffalo, catfish, bass,
despite the fish advisories, the waters laced with mercury.

85

VIRTUAL HORNETS
Keith Flynn

for Herbie Hancock

Sweet bee, declaring space, with your face
Upturned in the clatter and buzz, poised between
The giants and the flower children, you know
That dolphins dance but bear no sting, cannot fling
This dart, this Jazz, riding atop your wooden pistil,
Animal guts slicing this rush of air that surrounds
You like water with its swish and giggle, rhythmic
Chameleons, flashing like orchids, writhe underneath
Your menacing swing. What fine white space inside
Your weightless loop and wiggle, like the boundless
Inner surface of a lung, syncopated as de Kooning,
Plastic ranger dipping your elastic tail in the dripping
Moog, your golden wet and glimmering stare,
A winged mood going its own middle way.

ODE TO GRAVITY
Diane Gage

after Pablo Neruda

You
are the world's
greatest
lover
the soul
of attraction
every body
& every thing
caught
in your long
patient embrace
sourest lemon,
sweetest plum.

They say
you were born
dancing
that dancing
is the heart
of your secret
& wisdom.
See
how you amuse
the children

how
you win over
elders
to your point
of view
how you inspire
ingenuity
in scientists
bravado
in daredevils.

Every lucky day
you kiss
the soles of my feet
with the skin
of the earth
& at night
my whole body
knows your touch
there is no part
of my body
you are not constantly
caressing,
luring me
gradually
down.

Oh earth artist
master sculptor
you fashion
beautiful layers
of geological alchemies
absorb
& transform
mounds

of detritus
into seductions
of texture
bewitchments
of shadow
& glancing,
probing light.

You coax
tears from clouds
the wind
your comb
your brush
your earth-valet
the oceans and rivers
your boogie-woogie
mambo
cha cha
mamas
all gleaming
swish of skirt
flashing castanets.

Your playmates
the birds
laugh & chatter
in the toss
& glide
of their affair
with you
butterflies wink
bees hum
the endless symphony
of aerial flirtation
that humans try

to imitate
with constructed wings
parachutes
balloons.

But
however far
your reach
& influence
however grand
the scale
of your realm
you never fail
to touch
the smallest
& most humble
never neglect
to tuck
the tiniest
of seeds
into bed
to draw its minute legs
deeper
towards a hot heart
allowing
its slim bit of green
to reach up
to announce
yet another
vertical
miracle.

SPEEDY GONZALES, AN APPRECIATION

Rigoberto González

The mouse was brown. And I was brown.
He was a Gonzales. And I was a González.
We were both Mexican, though the Mexicans
I knew didn't wear sombreros or walk around in white.
Maybe in the old Pancho Villa movies
with peasants who couldn't grow mustaches.
When they rallied they blinded the screen like snow.
Their villages so different from the cartoon ghost towns
with a lone cantina and bored mice puffing on cigarettes,
all of them male. "What is it, a gay bar?" my father once asked.

Speedy, the only one who could outrun el Señor Gato,
embarrassed my father with his battlecries
¡Ándale, ándale, arriba, arriba! which made no sense.
"Who's the cat supposed to be? La migra?"
My father said. "No Mexican can run that fast."
Nor any mouse. A sharp snap in the middle of night
meant a rodent got its neck broken by the trap.
What did my mother use to entice it since here,
in our U.S. house, the only cheese I ever saw was on TV,
thick wedges that pointed to the mouths of cartoon mice.

Yet my father and I still watched side by side
as Speedy Gonzales bolted without losing his hat.
It was all make-believe anyhow, this strange México
where the poor had to take from the rich. We knew
about rising early for our meal, and cooking up
the swap meet pumpkins given out for free on Halloween.
No lazy Mexicans here, gringo pussycat, even if you peek
through the cracked window and catch us sitting there,
waiting for the only Spanish words we will hear on TV,
waiting for the mouse band to bring us music from so far away.

ODE TO MY TOYOTA
Kelle Groom

Through floorboard holes like open windows
on the road beneath my feet, through the back
seat windows that constantly slid down
as if cranked by invisible children, they came
for the mushrooms that grew in the carpet
lush from all the unrestricted rain, the diet of pink
liquid drizzle at the bottom of Pep Power cups
collected on the passenger side: roaches arriving
on their soundless fast feet, glossy palmetto
bugs big as a hand, and in the dark,
I always drove twitching, shaking my hair,
the overhead light burned out, music
stopped inside the radio of my 1974 Toyota,
and still she ran, the world's longest lasting car,
finally sold for a hundred dollars to a friend's husband
after he'd become lost in addiction to sex, contracted
AIDS, a beautiful man with blue jewel eyes, faceted
and cracked like ice, but perfect, a kind of sundial,
with a brightness that made it hard to hear his words,
to do anything but nod. He drove my car so far north,
everything froze, and covered in ice, in Minnesota
or Michigan, after years, the radio came on
like a person materializing beside him, and he called
his wife to tell her how he'd been driving, and someone
started to sing. He'd been scared at first, in the dark,
gone now, wherever the car has taken him.

ODE TO MY LEGS
Lola Haskins

Thank you for carrying me at great effort to mountains that gave me the view I saved in a box I concealed from him who would have taken all my boxes and piled them in the yard and struck a match, or fed them to the pigs that have grown large and refuse being scratched between the ears, so have sealed their deaths, their futures of hanging in smoke.

Thank you for sustaining me down dirty streets toward harbors where oil pools around the rusty hulls of freighters with Japanese names, whose sailors will never come out of the bars they rolled into late last night with their tongues like thirsty flags.

Thank you for not saying no to afternoons where young men dead for centuries eased me down on marble floors and had their way with me while I seethed under their black eyes, while I desired with every fire in my blood their ruffs and swords.

Thank you for granting me aisles of papaya heaped so tall that God was silent, silent also at the peaks of chiles dark red and shriveled, silent at the striped towers of shawls so various that rainbows would not have dared, silent even before the litanies of the rotten and buzzing: sandia, platano, mamey.

Thank you for letting me run with Glenn who could be my son, while he tells me about the doughnuts he's eaten and the car he wants to buy, which will be fast and black—and I've never wanted doughnuts or cars but how I crave their muscles and the sweat of their shirts, and how grateful I am as I slide my feet into socks and tie my shoes and go out to where white and purple lilies proffer what will close when the sun becomes too much, which is what I ask of you, legs, and what you have given me every time, generous, long-boned, and clean.

GAZE

Christopher Howell

I gaze through glass
at the red maple by the garage
and the bird feeder

empty of birds.
What is the meaning of life?
Cisco and Pancho are laughing

as they ride, flinging back
their sombreros. The ridiculous
and somber Lone Ranger

fills me with love.
My mother walks through wind
to the clothesline

and I am happily no one
I need to know
trotting up the path

between orchards in a blue
cowboy hat.
I gaze again. The clouds are silver

stallions above foothills of the Cascades
east of us. There's my mother
again, leaning down to pet the dog,

straightening, shading her eyes
to view the clouds, a stampede
of laundry-like meaning

at which she shrugs.

AWE TO ENNUI
Tom Hunley

The ceiling says, There's a rain-rinsed sky
above me, so beautiful, so blue
that it's hard to hang on and stay still.
Can't you feel it, Ennui? There's a Fourth of July
happening inside the professor's ribs,
if he will live it, if he will listen, if he'll lift his head.

The desk says I am not a pillow.
As an oak tree, it lived a long life
in the sun, in the open air, and one time
it stood by while a wounded hawk, mended
at last, scythed the night sky with its wings.
That tree, this desk, was the only witness
except for me, Awe, with my fixed dropped jaw.
The desk will speak to the professor in whatever
language desks and professors share,
if he remembers its syntax, if he listens, if he lifts an ear.

The student paper atop the professor's in-box
says, My name is Lindsay. I'm eighteen years old.
On commencement night cruising in my new Supra
I splintered a willow tree and totaled my graduation present.
I then spent two months in a coma. The paper concludes
It's always morning and I'm always being born.
I added that line myself, Ennui, and I'll tell you what:
I know that the professor will understand it, every word,
if he will read it, if he will listen, if he'll lift his brows.

NORTH OF BIG SUR
James Iredell

I am tired of California
emissions standards,
Jetta-driving wine connoisseurs
whining, hey bro
to the Valley floor, a quilt
of crops, a growing salad bowl
of lettuce and broccoli,
Mexicans dotting the patchwork
like croutons.
The fog wraps me in its serape,
the coils of a rattlesnake.
Yo soy Norteño. Yo soy
Californio. Yo soy
Montereño. I try but cannot speak
more than Taco
Bell Spanish: Yo quiero
a new commercial.
Fremont Peak stares
over the bay from beneath
the moon, its radio tower
broadcasting lies
into the fruit basket
of Monterey County.
Point Lobos, a wolf's mouth,
misty with sea water, has teeth
plaqued with barnacles.

Cannery Row, a squeaky glass
aquarium with clean tourists
swimming the sidewalks for mojitos
or novelty sea otter T-shirts.
The jellyfish imagine human reproduction.
May the crosses on the hills
above Santa Cruz play banjos
for the redwoods so that the sorrel
and miner's lettuce might carpet
the forest floor like the 1970s.
In Pajaro the birds sing canciones
for the little river
that floods strawberry
fields so that they grow
like Beatles songs.
Aromas smells of soccer and children.
In Carmel monks grow roses
and Mercedes in their gardens.
and pile them like driftwood.
Valley of Prunes, may your eucalyptus
shed leaves upon the fertile soil,
or boys ready for sacramentos,
or the Monterey County Jail blocks.
Coyote Bush, may you grow
tall and range across the ice plant.
Bing's Diner in Castroville
has closed and the empty railroad
car waits for travelers
to fill its booths
before driving south
to Los Angeles, below the valley
of heaven. Watsonville Mexicans
want hamburgers and work.
They sicken of tacos, waiting
on street corners for contractors

who pay in pizza.
Your dunes shrubbed by eucalyptus,
your fields strawberried red and green,
your streets picked by earthquakes.
The monarchs speckle Pacific Grove
demanding tax breaks
and parking spaces.
The pelicans at Elkhorn Slough
have out-fished the fishermen
and sharks. The waters are overrun
with thick green algae.
Mount Toro: your back is as a bull's,
round and thick-skinned,
brown as mud and bare
with thick potrero stands
spotted with Monterey manzanita.
St. Helena, your grapes moan
for higher wages and health insurance.
I squint in the California brome.
The Mediterranean barley catches
in my socks and itches my calves.
The rabbitsfoot grass, green
in May, has browned the hills to gold.
I'd surf to Capitola
on an ocean of women and beer.
Like a snake Highway 101 stretches
through the valley, a vein
pumping the blood of automobiles.
Clint Eastwood, your mayoral duties
went unnoticed. Don your cowboy hat
and toss away your name.
I hear of killer freshies at Sugar Bowl.
That is so extreme.
Let's go live at The Lake.
Everyone wants to live at The Lake.

Mostly because people would love
to say, "I live at The Lake,"
the Lake of the Sky, stolen fair.
I voted for the Governor.
He wants so badly to terminate
our open borders.
Let's build a wall across the desert
because this is Logical.
The Governor flexes his muscle
for the President.
I wrote a song about California.
It's called "California."
It goes a little something like this:
"California, California, California."
So imagery-full you can
visualize bikinis sporting
in furrowed fields, and rusted
Corvettes, their windshields shattered
along the Grapevine.
I will paint a picture of California
with all the colors in it,
then photograph my painting,
and chop the photo and the painting up
together and snort them, one big gagger,
a numbing choke all the way home.
I would float
into the arms of San Francisco
and a million hippies could break
my fall with their dreads when I come
crashing down so hard
you'd never think for a moment
that I'd ever left.

SORROWFUL ODE
Richard Jackson

I'm sorry for still loving you this way. I'm sorry for letting these words
lunge between us the way the wind does through a tiny knot of flame.
I'm sorry for letting them ferment the way the sun does each night.
There's no excuse, and yet, maybe I am not so sorry for still loving you
this way. I don't pay any attention to the way the filament in the bulb
glows for only a few seconds when the light goes out. It doesn't matter
to me that the river stores the city's lights only to sweep them downstream.

Sorry or not, I don't think there is anyone left in my soul. Therefore,
I am not so sorry for still loving you this way, the way a sunken boat
recalls its sail. Sometimes I think the heart is a beehive someone has
turned over. Sometimes it is a silkworm building its obscure cocoon.
There must be a few derelict constellations with no light to show us yet.
I'm sorry, but sometimes I also think you have created the night.
Other times I think you must have inhaled the breath of stars.

I'm sorry for loving you this way, for loving you still. Each memory
hollowed out the way water drips for centuries through a sandstone cave.
The ambulance siren slithering away through the streets but lingering on.
The wood frogs freezing themselves dry all winter to revive in Spring.
I'm sorry, but maybe the truest love is the most desperate. I'm sorry.
I'm not sorry. Sometimes I think these words rot like fallen fruit, and
sometimes I think you are the smell of rain that inhabits the air before a storm.

OBJECTS IN THIS MIRROR ARE CLOSER THAN THEY APPEAR

Richard Jackson

Because the dawn empties its pockets of our nightmares.
Because the wings of birds are dusty with fear.
    Because another war has eaten its way
    into the granary of stars. What can console us?

Is there so little left to love? Is belief just the poacher's
searchlight that always blinds us, and memory just
    the tracer rounds of desire? Last night,
    under the broken rudder of the moon, soldiers

cut a girl's finger off for the ring, then shot her and the boy
who tried to hide under a cloak of woods beyond their Kosovo
    town. Listen to me,—we have become words
    without meanings, rituals learned from dried

river beds and the cellars of fire-bombed houses.
Excuses flutter their wings. Another mortar round is
    arriving from the hills. How long would you say
    it takes despair to file down a heart?

When, this morning, you woke beside me, you were mumbling
how yesterday our words seemed to brush over the marsh
    grass the way those herons planed over
    a morning of ground birds panicking in their nests.

When my father left me his GI compass, telling me
it was to keep me from losing myself, I never thought
      where it had led him, or would lead me. Today,
      beside you, I remembered simply the way you eat

a persimmon, and thought it would be impossible for each
drop of rain not to want to touch you. Maybe the names
      of these simple objects, returning this morning
      like falcons, will console us. Maybe we can love

not just within the darkness, but because of it. Ours is
the dream of the snail hoping to leave its track on the moon.
      we are sending signals to worlds more distant
      than what the radio astronomers can listen for, and yet–

And yet, what? Maybe your seeds of daylight will take root.
Maybe it is for you the sea lifts its shoulders to the moon,
      for you the smoke of some battle takes the shape of a tree.
      On your balconies of desire, in your alleyways of touch,

each object is a door opening like the luminous face of
a pocket watch. Maybe because of you the stars, too,
      desire one another across their infinite,
      impossible distances forever, so that it is not

unthinkable that some bird skims the narrow sky where
the sentry fires have dampened, where the soldier, stacking
      guns in Death's courtyard, might look up, and remember
      touching some story he carries in his pockets, a morning

like this blazing through the keyholes of history, seeing not
his enemy but those lovers, reaching for each other, reaching
      towards any of us, their words splintering on the sky,
      the gloves of their hearts looking for anyone's hands.

A SUMMER WITHOUT ICE

Robin Leslie Jacobson

Oakland, California

Tonight she longs for something sturdier than a life raft,
some means of rescue she will have to imagine.
On the late late news, world scientists predict a summer without
ice—too late for banking on carbon credits or state-of-the-art
science. A whole ocean empty of what sank the Titanic.
No more reindeer or believing in Santa, she thinks. No more amazement.

Tonight a gas tanker slams into a guardrail in the MacArthur Maze, meant
for lower speeds. Hundred-foot flames. Three a.m., when life rafts
most often fail to rescue sleepers tossing in titanic
dreams. When death most often turns the living into imaginary
voices. But the freeway is empty, the driver breaks free. Life mimics art—
he hails a Friendly Cab. At the ER the cabbie says he should go without

paying his fare. Just go! Let he who is without
sin, the cabbie must be thinking, the crash-and-burn in the maze meant
to wake everyone up. She is still up, sleeplessness echoing in her arteries
like the voices of emergency workers calling out at the scene. No life raft
for her tonight. At this hour hardly anyone is awake, she imagines,
watching the news, then remembers the other half of the world, titanic

in its burning—holocaust and love. But the melted freeway is titanic
enough for her to navigate—the driver, the cabbie, the workers without
sleep. Ones make it possible to feel the millions. This way she can imagine

A'isha, 6 (an Iraqi's name and age pinned on her at a protest), her amazement
shaky but holding, holding the little girl like a life raft.
Imagine A'isha is still alive tonight. This way six billion hearts

keep time together better than one atomic clock. This way the heart
to live keeps beating in her chest. Suicide seems impossible, titanic,
not meant for little girls strapped to explosives. And life rafts
seem possible even in the worst of circumstances—little girls without
homes, a summer without ice. Tonight amazement
keeps the vigil with her like an imaginary

friend. She imagines the freeway whole again, imagines
the driver unburned, the truck still holding him like a heart.
No breaker, breaker. He gets where he's going unamazed.
And tonight the world doesn't seem impossible, titanic—
just A'isha alive at 6, a cabbie in the right place at the right time without
needing another fare. Love is the best life raft,

she finally dreams, her life rafting through brainstorms, a maze
of nerves. Imagination waits in the space between endings. Without,
the Titanic always sinks. Within, she can rescue one girl in a heartbeat.

TINY SPARROW FEET
Michael Johnson

It's calm.
Too quiet.
My clear plastic bowl
serves as my bird feeder.
I don't hear the distant
scratching, shuffling
of tiny sparrow feet,
the wing dances, fluttering, of a hungry
morning's lack of big band sounds.
I walk tentatively to my patio window,
spy the balcony with detective eyes.
I witness three newly hatched
toddler sparrows, curved nails, mounted
deep, in their mother's dead, decaying back.
Their childish beaks bent over elongated,
delicately, into golden chips, and dusted yellow corn.

JUNKYARDING THROUGH THE GREAT MORENO VALLEY

Janine Joseph

S. was always looking for a carburetor
and I'd hang around
to get some sleep on the bench
seat of his Ford. When I was awake
and not browsing the glove compartment,
I'd help comb the rust edging the lots,
finding nothing shaped like a such-
and-such all day. We'd split up
—he called it double-timing—
and I'd poke around at alternators and engines
under the corrugated hoods.
If I got lucky, a cat or possum would
skedaddle out a trunk, or I'd find
a cassette we'd jammed to
at the skating rink a few years back.
Once when I was leaning against the open
door of a stripped jeep, he proposed
with a pipe clamp too big for any
of my fingers. I still wore it around,
every so often forgetting what it was
and calling it a gasket.
We were always getting it wrong,
he and I. He'd tell me to look for
serpentine belts, but to stay away from

the rattlesnakes, and I'd come back
swinging an inner tube or two on my arms.
It was good.
            Sure, not much
happened, but those things
we'd holler one after the other
across the junkyards, weekend after weekend,
well, they became something
like a language passed between us, our own
long American sentence.

AS YOU BREATHE IN THE SLOUCHING

George Kalamaras

In this city of tombs, you feel incredibly alive.
And all your past, the kisses, the defeats.

Even the clutching in the dark. Where are they now?
The Mogul tomb is a brown river moon thrust up into light.

You see the tomb and feel a scrag of the Jamuna River.
Listen: one carp plus one carp always equals one gold carp.

Brilliantly, trees are swimming through afternoon Delhi sky.
All that blue remains as only an outline for peepal leaves.

You stepped out of one moon and entered another.
And everyone else believes that they cannot fly?

Not everyone, you realize, as you breathe in the slouching
of those who swat mosquitoes and fear their next life.

Malaria now, or some later incarnation as a pig?
One death plus one death is said to equal a jar of Bombay Gin.

One mosquito net above the bed is enough to culch the moon
of all its waste, drag the river for minnow scum and shad.

Not always, you realize, as you drink in Lodi Gardens.
Blue peacock fire blazing the glaze of sun on red sandstone.

And all your past, the sorrowful kisses, the joyous defeats?
All that glorious death, and you're still alive.

PHENOMENOLOGY OF THE VANISHING HORIZON
Gerry LaFemina

Tortola, B.V.I.

Because a life is laden with departures,
I stopped at the airstrip to watch another 737 approach,
twin lights barely aglow in Carribean heat,
its metallic torso almost graceful
      —how many tons in the air?

Lowering steady offshore,
      its jets issued a flotilla of spray
which diffracted the light
& then it was done

but for the engines' distracted roar, the rush of wind I knew
was the wing flaps turning upward.

Even from that distance I could feel moisture.

~

From certain points here you look east at nothing but sea & sky,

the problems of latitude & longitude. To the west

the humped back of islands
dropped like a child's toys, some so close
you can see resplendent flowering trees: magenta, orange, violet blurs.

Beaches shouldering surf. Yes,
there are always boats, white bodies bobbing on their lines with
tides.

~

A small shark swims in the shallows. Truly,
it's beautiful: the length of my arm
from fingertips to elbow, its body a mix of glimmer
& shade. It follows the shore

sputters in a wave's waning moment
then shimmies away
                        toward deeper water. In the shadow play of
breakers,
I lose sight of it.

~

What's a wave but an ever-changing curve,
a mathematical anomaly?

~

Because these islands are isolated
like aesthetes in their chambers, praying, many are named after
saints;

~

like churches I attended years ago,

smell of incense rubbed into pews. I learned
to genuflect & mark a cross
on four points of the body—both shoulders, forehead, chest: places
            where sin may lie.

Tonight, slight spray of sea as I walk the shoreline:

the Southern Cross like four moments of holy water.

~

Again wave sound which lulls us to sleep
& wave sound which calls us awake.

I walk the shore at night, slim waves
                              shatter around my feet—

doilies of foam. Overhead: a blinking red airplane.

Water & sky both dark so it's as if there's no horizon,

what Zen masters call non-duality—
the universe without boundaries: moonless,

freckles of star,
              boat light shimmering dimly below.

~

I want to write a phenomenology of the wave shattering
& reforming, the phenomenology of light
in orange crests rippled with shadow.

~

Dawn divides the sky & earth once more, reaffirming
what we know.
                    A local works with homemade lobster traps
wood, mesh & rope,

then drops one offshore, only a homemade buoy marking it
—plastic bleach jug—bobbing so close I could swim there.

I used to watch men at South Beach

laboring with crab traps: hauling the ropes hand over hand,
plucking crustaceans gently
then plopping them in buckets. I'd pause there on the pier
as they harvested,
                              some for restaurants, some for dinner.

I'd trot to the pier's end behind my mother's boyfriend,
he who tried to teach the rod & reel,
who tried to chart for me the territories of manhood.

He's disappeared into those years . . . .

I want to write the phenomenology of the vanishing
horizon. I want
to write the phenomenology of this self.

How are those two things different?

~

Early morning rain—
                    tropical, torrential—
                                        for only a few minutes

then sun converting puddles to steam.

These islands were once magma. I know this.
Liquid to solid/liquid to gas.
I sweat. I breathe. I can rub my fingers together—sacred
        truths of physical science:

no prayer but the solace of facts.

~

The sharks that crash against the lobster cages
are sometimes pulled up in rope tangles. Some are killed

with a blow to the head,
& served in restaurants to tourists like us;

others are released flopping into the sea again.

I see one swimming in the shoals at dawn—
it returns splashing toward deeper water
as the tide slumps,
                shark gills pumping for breath.

I watch it, silver in the silvery water, till it seems to vanish.
I almost know where it's going.

MIDDLE-AGED AT THE MILLENNIUM

Peggy Landsman

With apologies to T.S. Eliot

I have no plan of action, only memory...

Grew up in the sixties when we thought we knew
Exactly how to change the world, all we had to do:

Organize the masses, hold teach-ins at school,
Pressure our officials, sign an early truce,

Love one another, be spontaneous,
Lose bourgeois hang-ups, be impetuous...

The times, at times, were too tumultuous—
We were, at times, their tool.

TREES

Dorianne Laux

Wind shuffles through oak, pine, liquid amber, elm.
I can't name their shades of green. I can't know them
like I want to. Can't translate their whispers.
They have thrown down their shadows like old scarves.

Birds live inside them like small beating hearts.
The bugs, savage, tunnel through to their fiery cores.
They drip bright skeins of moss. They are trellises
for the killing ivy, the rampant kudzu's suckered feet.

The cardinal's red wings disappear in their leaves,
leaves shaped like hearts, boats, needles, flutes,
combs and cradles. They live a long time, generations
of bees swarm and return. They wear lightning

strikes like dark badges, smudged shields.
They branch and branch from their limbs until
there's too much of them to comprehend. I love them
without warning. They have traveled a long way
to stand before me in their crippled dignity.

JAPANESE AMERICAN NATIONAL MUSUEM CONCERT

Carol Lem

He breathes into his bamboo flute
while the photos and objects of internment
breathe back. Silence enters the first note
as he searches for the still point
between the man, a pail of water in one hand,
his daughter on the other, and the occasional
tourist pausing at a display case,
"Where is Manzanar?"

He is playing to the distant cry of a deer,
so solitary in his forest of sounds
he doesn't see the woman in the front row
whose father's flute rests on the table,
the one thing he had left to teach others with
in camp. Five empty holes stare back.

ODE TO BOMBS

Alexander Long

I'm thinking that whistling far off in the distance
                                      there
Is something to hum along with. It's history's
                        little anthem,

And we hum its one note as long as we can breathe
It through, don't we....
                  And when the whistling stops,

There's no city of fire, no blackened glass,
                            no girders

Curved around and through the village's last and useless horse.

There's only a story, the truest one, that no one
                           tells, or can.

So, go on, drop
        the landscape into tidily shattered lines that drop
                                  themselves,

Then, look up
        at clouds that neither gather nor hover,

But simply are, are scattering from smoke,
                                                                              are almost celebrating

themselves,

Their invisible, inevitable dissolution,

As the planes go on bestriding each other,

And the glass, the girders, the horse, the village
                                                                                                    let go

Of themselves, and why not? I'm thinking...
                                                                                                    I'm thinking

Ecstasy, a loss
                                  of breath, a hovering, some alley

In a corner of Baghdad where two teenagers

Feel each other up, and the whistles multiply and amplify,
                                                                                                              why not,

As a little fire
                              spreads from home to home, and why

Not have the boy strike a match, which makes the girl
                                                                                                    giggle,

To light his cigarette, for this is the custom of adults....

I'm thinking he calls her Oh Donna and Runaround Sue, and he
                                                                                                              drags

And hums and breathes the smoke into her,

                                        where
every thought
Is permissible and rebellious, and hums along,

inaudibly,

Goodbye goodbye goodbye...

WHAT WE LIVE FOR
Perie Longo

"Every time I write a poem
I fall in love with it..."
—Anonymous fourth grader

...the musk that opens static ducts and the press
of pine needles soft on the small of the back, his eyes
full of each inch of you, the breath in—his,
the breath out—yours, how the hushed forest awoke
when your song scattered the meadowlarks
into the blank blue sky, your quivering the water's pulse
against the banks. Then there's the writing of it,

how Chinese white pear blossoms catch in the wind
like snowflakes, settle on the tips
of winter's brown twigs. With your favorite pen in hand,
the smooth one whose ink flows gently across the flesh
of the page, words start to come, one against
the other, small kisses lined up, soon you're swimming
in them, with them, you pull back, they chase you, catch you,
together you trace back roads of memory as the lover's fingers

remind you what is true, there will be no truce until
you focus, give your all, release. Child, the poem you birthed
folded in your pocket is what we live for, what saves us,
drives us mad, these words we may one day die for.

ODE TO VEGAS
Alison Luterman

There's a hole in my soul that nothing can fill.
You too? Let's meet up in Vegas,
because life is hard; that's why we need this place
where a retired waitress from Arizona,
weather-beaten as a beach house
in hot pants and a halter top,
platinum curls and turquoise eye shadow,
can sit in front of a one-armed bandit all night,
pulling on that lever like it was her dead ex-husband.
Everything dies in the end,
but the party keeps going
as long as you can keep up with it,
So have some ten-dollar steak! Have a beer
or more coffee at 4 a.m.
and tip whatever's left in your pockets.
In this light, you look great;
the stars are on dimmer switches
so they won't hurt us by being so damn distant
and unattainable. The moon's overcome.
We don't need no stinking Nature
with its mud and dung beetles,
its rot and decay.
We have piped-in fountains
that undulate to opera in the middle of the desert,
man-made breasts that rival the Pyramids,

because Nature's game is rigged—
the house always wins.
So lean over the green baize table
and watch your destiny ricochet free of its story.
Be Queen for a Day
or a week, as long as your cash holds out.
Honey, here's hoping
you can change your fortune
even up to the last minute.

THE JOY-BRINGER

Thomas Lux

breaks the light through the oak leaves at dawn.
The joy-bringer injects the red bird's red.
The joy-bringer brings the green, lets the cup runneth over
into a saucer, from which you can sip.
Gives fish to the river, the river the fish.
If by two inches you avoid a piano
falling on your head
and later at the hospital fall in love with the doctor
who removes a few splinters
of ivory and black piano lacquer
from your left calf: the joy-bringer
arranged that. Also the chilled artesian water
spilling from a pipe only two inches above the ground,
from which you drank on your hands and knees,
on a few boards or branches, you bowed in the muck and drank
that sweet cold reaching-up,
you drank among the skunk cabbage, ferns, a small brook
at your back: again, guess what,
the joy-bringer! In fact, let us praise
the joy-bringer for these seven
things: 1) right lung, 2) left lung, 3) heart, 4) left brain,
5) right brain, 6) tongue, 7) the body to put them in.
Thank you, joy-bringer!
And thanky, thanky too for just-mown hay
cut an inch from its roots
to bleed its perfume into the air!

SKYWALKER

Sebastian Matthews

for Ali, on her birthday

You should see it: out in the field, a gang
of waxwings swarming low over corn stubble
converging in the field, perching in the trees,
screeches metal sheets rubbing over the river.
They swoop in the sky as a single organism:
Escher dance of white body to black, one huge bird
in flight now a thousand on the ground—waving,
wings in unison, a distinct whouck like laundry
snapped taut as they turn and bank in the late
afternoon light. Have I ever told you how
in the airport my father ran into David Thompson,
our favorite basketball player? "Skywalker"—
the skinny rocket-legged forward who dunked
on the heads of slow-footed 7-footers. They'd bumped
into each other in line for coffee, he'd always say,
sitting down for a few moments of light banter.
Two elegant, tall men—the poet and the athlete.
I was thinking about this the other day when I found
an old faded red-white-and-blue ABA basketball
trapped in a tree branch, bobbling in the river's hands.
I was brooding on my father, who died on this day
nine years ago, so fished the ball out and brought it
to you. Can you decipher this childhood talisman,
made slick first by hands and hardcourt then water?
Will you help me bury it in these woods by the river?

When I return to the corn the day is newly written
and the waxwings have given way to crows marauding
in the trees, lost in a mystery play, a floating crap game
of complaint, my old friends. Here's what the men
must have said. First: "How do you dance along
that thin strip of baseline like that, brother?" Then:
"How do you sketch words in the sky so birds come
together to rant inside the clouds?" "It's easy:
I'm just a reporter standing at the edge of the field,
waiting out the tornado." "That's funny, sometimes
I'm a hawk swooping, others a bassline pulsing.
The ball disappears in my hands." "Yes, yes, it's as if
vision goes so fast into its next correct place
that you meet it coming back." When you jump up,
you are really two forces converging" "Passion is all
the body needs for intelligence." I say: "Sometimes
the wind hinders, sometimes the wind helps."
Skywalker laughs. Then: "I'll miss my flight."
Dad: "Good luck tonight. Don't let Dr. J go off
in the third." I turn the bend in the river, dog out
ahead on the prowl, your face conjured,
and blow out as inspired breath a kiss to you.

MORNING LINES WITH HORSES RUNNING THROUGH

Sebastian Matthews

We have made our way up the slope of the field,
our school of students disturbing a flock of geese,

forcing them to rise as one ragged unit,
crescendo of flapping wings, and are walking

up the lane to the famous barns. At least twice
a month a group like us arrives here, pilgrims

in search of any slight connection to history,
hoping to step back into the mountain air

artists inhabit when they come together
open-hearted and serious about work.

Black Mountain College now a camp, a music
festival, a summer Eden circling

a man-made lake. At the top of the hill
two horses burst from behind trees and sprint

around the corner. We're in their world now,
and they gallop at us with what can only

be named happiness. Was it Albers who made
that elegant design in the barn's back wall?

A student wants to know: How did they learn
to do this? The silo tiled like a sacred tower,

Orazco-style frescos at the base
of the study building, its corrugated siding

peeling from the years. One horse
chews on the fringe of Katie's shawl;

the other lets Carrie and Griffin
pet his thick fur. Soon they will tire

of us, this empty-handed group
already thinking of the next thing.

Alex and Mike run ahead, flinging
themselves down the hill. Sam lingers

by the barns, eyeing the handiwork
around him. We make our way

to the vans. The geese have dispersed.
The blue sky our only text.

OHIO

Derek Mong

an etymology

      comes to us from oh hello
Which some believe to mean "I am in a state
Of abbreviated greeting," i.e.: she blinks, I wave,
She winks before the Erie snow

Can melt upon my glasses. Other Ohio
Examples: gravel strafed by headlights, a shield
Of green seen from a cockpit. Explanation two
Contends Ohio grew into a double ode

From a sole, initial blooper: uh oh—
Oh oh, oh ooooh my home can speed into a love
Cry or a lyric! Is such ecstasy dubious
When its first note foreshadows

Its finale? Like adolescents and army time, zeroes
Frame all of Ohio's encounters. In fact, some think
We split off from a whisper which went creasing
Through the prairie: I ow a— O hi o—

Sisters till a glacier cleaved them? Oh
No, not so. Ohio's as indivisible as amber waves
From rusted pickups. For instance, I have traced
My state's origin back to this abiding sorrow:

It's night, I'm driving with my windows
Down, the cold's encircling my collar. I swear
The earth below me begins to swell and drop   133
Like three syllables stretched into four low

Then lower letters. The sky goes blank with snow.
I drove and drove into the pages of Ohio.

AMERICA,

Martin Moran

America, if I could I would tighten my eyes to the smoke
between your ribs and wake up in your heart   if I could
find you now I'd tell you we are but a broken ornament
swinging on a fraying string   we are a dripping city, the sweat
that smears the phonebook ink   America, save your traffic
for another hour, love your oil mill and boxcar, breathe your "can't,":
instead, as fuel, dare to sing your limits from the ashfields
and the quarries   in Franklin, Indiana, your nuclear froths
like mad animal, your Lakeshore strobe a bourbon and the slat
of passing freight, your live oak, a Georgia shackle –
to all of it, tonight, wrap yourself in Kansas flag: ad astra
per aspera   tonight, let the reapers in the forty bathe in star.

UPROOTED

Indigo Moor

It took all our weight to drag the chain
over the stump, my brother

and I heaving links heavy enough
to strangle hope. Our hands lost

in grandfather's big work gloves,
slick grass betrayed our bare feet.

The tractor vibrated low. Hummed,
screeched, and began humming again.

Smoke marbled gray the blue morning.
Where we once played king-of-the-hill

on the stump's weathered face, we now
played Judas with an iron-linked kiss.

Grandfather spat Red Fox
tobacco, feathered the clutch once

to tighten the noose. The engine leaned,
a runner into wind, as the chain notched,

deep into the wood, a lover's
embrace gone shockingly wrong.

The stump shuddered, groaned, wrenched
from the earth and tilted skyward.

I don't know what we expected.
There were no secrets.

No ghosts. No magic. Only
naked roots torn from the earth.

We stood with hands at our sides,
lost in the tremor song of earth,

all of us, broken like a promise.
Air so raw, it scratched our lungs.

Days passed, until once more we
circled the stump. Each of us, secretly

hoped enough time had passed
for the love that married this stump

to earth to slip away. We then laid
axe to wood and released the rings.

DUDS

Jack Myers

When one of our cherry bombs didn't go off
we'd call it a dud and gingerly approach it.
What kid could run away from something
that promised to blow up? Here in America
we're still stuck now between epiphany and disappointment,
boring ourselves into the bedrock of uncertainty,
our heads going off like promises into the wild blue yonder,
certain we could still be anything we wanted.

NIGHT SKIERS
Katherine Northrop

Now they are falling
       through a system of dreams—and appearing

out of the pines, they descend

       on trails blue & luminous as bones
photographed in the body, and what's clear

       from a distance is the revelation
of miniatures: they have gone up

in order to fall, as do the names of those
       we no longer know, as do headlights crossing the wall
of a kitchen beyond which the wind

ruffles rows of dead corn, and the skiers

dropping easily this evening through the lines of structure—trees,
       lifts—pause once or twice, hinged

in a parallel turn, but do not care
       —not now—to listen to those
faint scratches in the buried dirt—so they land,

and cutting in, carrying on, are they not
beautifully suited? —to descend like this,

returning again to the base
        and to the lover who is half-
imagined, and waiting there.

THE PURE BEAUTIES
Katherine Northrop

There they go—flying
    out of our hands

and for all the world looking like our memory
of leaves turned on the pond into boats
and then, of the boats themselves,

the horizon's white sails
disappearing, and steadily.

There they go—the pure beauties—
    tra la la,

each one perfectly alone
as a balloon is, as a small child,

they who never even knew of us
standing here in love
with the boats, our hearts, and losing them.

MUSCAT SUNDOWN
Naomi Shihab Nye

Young men erase the day's prints,
raking sand.

Five hundred netted sardines—
a sheen of final breaths hovers above waves.

Over there, Iran,
India three hours to the right...
None of the couples at this hotel
seem to speak to one another.
But they all love to read.

We're carrying burdens named for corporations,
dead friends, the father whose blood
ran through a machine for three difficult years...

Call for praying wraps around
each tiny ruffled head of waving grass...
Fountains. Fires lit in giant pots.

Parents shimmering inside our strides and bones.
Can't shake them out whatever we do.

After everything, smooth gray stones
cupped in a palm.

I would have loved
to walk here with you.

SANCTUARY

Elise Paschen

*[After the War of 1812], about fifty forts were planned, stretching from
Maine to Louisiana, with Key West being chosen . . . because of its
strategic position near important shipping lanes.
—Fort Zachary Taylor State Historic Site by C.G. Chambers*

I

Down past gunrooms, above the ocean swells,
protected by the reef, we track the sun
take its last plunge. I lead you by the hand.
A bagpipe keens across wide-open beach,
while three couples, yards apart, swear and swear.
Beneath the balustrades of the aged fort,
the armament is buried deep–the Parrott
rifles, Rodmans, Columbiads–encased
in sand. The couples on the sand repeat
their lines this New Year's Eve before the sun,
a cannon ball, tumbles into the sea.

II

Yellow Fever ravaged the fort in 1862.
Dusk now, new year, mosquitoes swarm. A welt
forms on our daughter's arm. Stepping through ruins
of rock, we spy remains of earlier weddings–
champagne flutes, paper plates, a trail of tulips.
Tracking the march, she scoops up petals, shards

or vows, to carry home. "Would your child eat
a slice of wedding cake?" the caterer asks.
(A cake buried beneath orchids and roses.)
Our three-year-old smiles yes, but as we exit,
I turn to see she's swallowing red blooms.

III

We build our fort. Towering tall, you stretch
the sheet taut, high above our heads. The children
burrow under pillows. Let's keep our vows.
Each night, flashlight in hand, we read aloud
more pages from weathered books. Blockade-running
schooners, coasting sea lanes, never attacked
this harbor. Seeking sanctuary under
the sheets, our brood takes cover while the thunder
discharges like artillery. We sleep
beneath blankets, stone, and mortar, unarmed,
the doors of our houses, unlocked, wide open.

ODE TO CONTRACTORS POSSESSING VARIOUS LEVELS OF EXPERIENCE

Alison Pelegrin

This one's a shout out to the git-r-dones,
the crowd since Katrina most idolized
and sucked up to—semi-nude roofers,
hard hatters, electricians, tree doctors,
Ditch Witch pilots dwelling in tent cities
or, like our lumberjacks, the Dollar General
parking lot. A round of drinks and first pick
of the MREs for you. Look—one thing
I've learned is what you had to do, you did.
They roughed it, and my hubby pimped me when
he had me with my sweet voice make the calls.
Soon they came in pairs, like yin and yang,
one to chain smoke in the truck, the other
to get paid—in our case three grand up front
before Tangipahoa's understudies
of beanpole-rotund Rosencrantz and Guildenstern
would aim their crowbars at the fouled Sheetrock.
With no other prospects we hired them
on the spot, feeling at once swindled
and spared on that first day and then the next
when nothing happened until dusk, and then
it came down all at once—skeleton walls
and Sheetrock ready to float before we could
line up shingles or a roofer. Sometimes

the vision doesn't translate to the page.
I'm not even sure I'm mad with them
for soaking brushes in my Calphalon
roasting pan and deciding we'd be fine
if they used the toilet as an ashtray.
Boys will be boys. They finished soon enough.
Maybe because we were nearing the end
I liked the last ones best, Scientologists
out of Lafayette that we hired away
from a neighbor. I learned to barter with
this crew, longnecks for the long lost secrets
of the split-jamb door. We had a routine
going. Morning call at six in our kitchen,
coffee and chicory, kiss the shakes goodbye.
One day we had the photo albums out
looking for a background shot of where
the plastered over phone jack used to be.
Like children, like the rest, they moved along
and never call. A fiction, what I knew so well.
No proof but dirty thumbprints and memory
of their tattoos which slurred, "We're into knives."
A broken record, the blue lines of their body art—
dagger, dagger, dagger, dagger, heart.

STILL MISSING THE JAYS
Stanley Plumly

Then this afternoon, in the anonymous
winter hedge, I saw one. I'd just climbed,
in my sixty-year-old body—with its heart
attacks, kidney stones, torn Achilles tendon,
vague promises of ulcers, various subtle,
several visible permanent scars, ghost-
gray hair, long nights and longer silences,
impotence and liver spots, evident
translucence, sometime short-term memory loss—
I'd just climbed out of the car and there
it was, eye-level, looking at me, young,
bare blue, the crest and marking jewelry
penciled in, smaller than it would be
if it lasted but large enough to show
the dark adult and make its queedle
and complaint. It seemed to wait for me,
watching in that superciliary way
birds watch too. So I took it as a sign,
part spring, part survival. I hadn't seen a jay
in years—I'd almost forgotten they existed.
Such obvious, quarrelsome, vivid birds
that turn the air around them crystalline.
Such crows, such ravens, such magpies!
Such bristling in the spyglass of the sun.

Yet this one, new in the world,
softer, plainer, curious. I tried
to match its patience, not to move,
though when it disappeared to higher ground,
I had the thought that if I opened up my hand—

ECLOGUES

Dawn Potter

Look, oxen now bring home their yoke-suspended ploughs,
And the sun, going down, doubles growing shadows; But I
burn in love's fire: can one set bounds to love?
—Virgil

I

The lovage is the shade
of Lincoln green in Sherwood,
stealthy green, its leaves sharp-tongued
and leathery and rude.

Even in the garden it is safe
from fortune hunters, its display
of riches cool and well restrained,
like yours today.

All hints I send to you are wrong,
misheard, or undergone
in tears. Long for me again.
Pour out your crazy thrush's song,

screel a hawk's lament three times,
or drum a grouse-beat in the pines.
Then in the lovage, hide your sign,
buried in the leaves, near mine.

II

A marriage worth of minutes we've stood
side by side, staring into the hooded depths
of your 1984 Dodge Ram pickup truck,
watching the engine chitter and die
for no apparent reason. I feel a crazy,
ignorant joy: here we go again, sweetheart,
struggling in harness over yet another
crappy mystery. Do you? I can't say I'll ever
know one way or the other what your thoughts
will do, though twenty years ago I made you cry
when I dumped you for the jerk down the hall,
and I'll never get over it, the sight of you,
cool autocrat, in tears for a dumb girl
who happened to be me.

Now I'm the one who cries all the time,
you're the one not walking away from me
down the hall. Just the same, you imagine
walking away, I'm sure of it; maybe when you're
dragging another snow-sopped log to the chainsaw
pile, or we're curled in bed waiting for a barred owl
to stammer in the pines, the barn dog shouting back
like a madwoman. It's not that being here
is misery; it's more like marriage is too much
and not enough at the same time: the trees crowd us
like children, our bodies betray a fatal longing.
What's left for us, at forty, but dismay
till labor shakes us back into our yoke.

Work, work, that puritan duty—yet
how beautiful the set of your shoulders
when you heave a scrap of metal siding
into the trash heap. Our bodies linger

this side of lovely, like flowers under glass.
We drive ourselves to endure; on my knees
in the hay mow, stifled and panting,
I plant bale after bale in place: you toss,
you toss, I shove, I shove. We keep pace,
patient and wordless; the goats in their pen
blat irritably. In the yard our sons quarrel.
Mourning doves groan in the eaves.
Long hours ahead, till our job is done
and another begins.

Hunting scattered chickens in the bug-infested dew:
I watch you crouch along the scrubby poplar edge,
then circle back between the apple trees,
white hen skittering ahead, luminescent in the shabby
dark. Suddenly she drops her head and sits,
submissive as a girl. You've got her now; tuck up her feet
and carry her back home, then squat to mend the ragged fence.
A breath of sweat rises from your sunburnt neck,
salt and sweet. My love. Marry me, I say. You cast
an eye askance and shrug, I did. How odd it seems
that this is where we've landed: chasing chickens
through the woods at twilight, humid thunder rumpling
the summer sky, dishes washed, a slice of berry pie left
cooling on the counter. I've been saving it for you.

   III

All the long day, rain
pours quicksilver
down the blurred glass.
gardens succumb to forest,

half-ripe tomatoes cling
hopelessly to yellow vines,
cabbages crumple and split,
but who cares?

Let summer vanish,
let the tired year
shrink to the width
of a cow path,

soppy hens straggle
in their narrow yard,
and every last leaf
on the maples redden,

shrivel, and die.
Nothing needs me,
today, but you,
sweet hand,

cupping the bones
of my skull. Alas,
poor Yorick, picked clean
as an egg.

How rich we grow,
bright sinew and blood,
my eyes open, yours
blue.

IV

Play "Sister Morphine" four or five times an hour,
sleet jittering the window, and what is it about that song

yanking the chain so tight I have to cover my eyes
before walls collapse? A lover can set bounds to love,

but then, is it still love, or some kinder emotion?
Trollope's married ladies esteem their ample lords;

but look at crazy Bradley Headstone, he doesn't
esteem Lizzie one bit, though he loves her

like a man from hell.
The novels say I'm reaching the prime of life

when I ought to forget about skin by firelight,
but I've always been a sucker for desire, I can't stop now

just because my friends have marriageable daughters.
Girls these days, they don't grow up watching Virginia

Woolf stir the soup, Juliet behind the barn dying for love.
What girl wants to be Virginia-thinking-of-Juliet anymore?

You're stuck with me, dear boy, pockets full of rocks,
though at least the river's frozen, no drownings till spring.

You'll have to give up the ghost and let me love you;
it's the best I can do, this dark age.

ODE TO DOUBT
Dorine Preston

Muscle of boa, you turn
smooth as cognac stilled
fifty years in the throat.
You muffle hard outlines
under your skirts,
offer a gray handkerchief
to each certainty.
Behind the civility of veils—
what manners! You understand
how vulgar clarity can be.
At your discretion,
the lampshade's tassels.
Yours, the axe swung wide.
You own the dog afloat
on the ocean, the blurred print
on the dog's sodden collar.
You shake the hand
that finds a cold canary,
burning lung that must inhale.
Smudge-mouthed last child
left in the parking lot.
Dead horse, middle fork,
gloved hands in hair.

ODE TO A CHILDHOOD PHOTOGRAPH

Bill Rasmovicz

Little freak. Little Narcissus who can't reach
the mirror yet, your foot
stuck in the commode. I don't even recognize you,
that teepee on your hand-me-down jacket,
your hair blackened by the coal cellar.
Who made you pose
like the neighbor's garage-sale taxidermy?
Was it the nuns dragged you there by your ear?
Did they nail you to the seat?
Who's got the knife in your side?
Who told you to smile like that?
Mr. Purveyor of Pissing Out the Window,
your complexion the orange glow of twilight
from the penitentiary. Is that your chest or mine
discharging now like shots from the guard tower?

CLARA'S VISION
William Reichard

Appalachian Trail

We drove for hours across terrain
I couldn't recognize; through
small towns with landscapes that read:
church, church, feed store, church,
past ramshackle houses that looked
as if they'd been pulled from
antique photographs: shoeless children
running through yards, old-looking
young women working
stern-faced on front porches.
We arrived near sunset,
when the light was gently capping
each ridge, cutting the edges
of rocks in red, pink, gray.
I didn't know what heaven was,
but perhaps this was it:
clouds sweeping gravel paths;
granite disappearing, then reappearing,
in the mist; small peaks poking out of
miniature white mountains within mountains.
The air was thin. I thought I might faint.
You pointed along the serpentine curve
of the path and told me it went
all the way up to Canada.
How far was that? How many
lifetimes would it take to traverse

that distance? Since I'd met you,
I'd only wondered, more and more,
how one can come to be saved,
I mean truly saved, not the
down-on-your-knees, begging
to be forgiven saved, but the kind
where we each come to know ourselves
—radiance and repulsion aside—
just simply to know ourselves.
I thought you'd found that
and I wanted it too.
As the sun set, the path began
to fade into an impenetrable darkness.
You said we'd hike the trail
one day and I believed you.
Then, back to the truck
for the long ride home.
I didn't know then what heaven was,
but I wanted to believe you did.

DURING THE LAST TWO WEEKS OF HIS LIFE, HE WROTE ONLY THE LAST LINES OF POEMS
Jack Ridl

I

the stars, lost in the half light of evening.

II

giving us only a noun and the time to understand it.

III

after the taxi, after the end of the affair.

IV

like the slow ruin of his own small town.

V

and God? Lost somewhere in the bread section.

VI

wind, three medieval priests, a puppet, and a wedding dress.

VII

the bus.

VIII

window, pouring out the last of the anonymous gin.

IX

not the cow, not the fence post, not even the back door.

X

knew the rest, but kept the pile beside her desk, adding to it when it snowed.

XI

amid the holiness of snails.

XII

later. Then he juggled a scarf, an orange ball, and his flute.

XIII

was it the rain, was it the ontology of morning?

ELLIS ISLAND
Karen Rigby

This poem is a photo of Ellis Island:
a gray square torn from an album
shadowed with sleeping faces.

This photo taped inside your piano
speaks a language not even
the drowned glove remembers.

This piano is an ocean of hammers
between a chill January morning
and a steamer crossing the Atlantic.

This ocean glints from the razor
your father sewed to his hatband
after fighting in Mallorca.

This razor hungers for bread
the color of teeth before whole
neighborhoods vanished.

This bread breaks in the name
of the gunsmith, the thresher,
the seamstress, the carpenter.

This name is a pebble inside you.
A petal darkening by the hour.
An animal odor on your tongue.

BORDER LINES
Alberto Ríos

A weight carried by two
Weighs only half as much.

The world on a map looks like the drawing of a cow
In a butcher's shop, all those lines showing
Where to cut.

That drawing of the cow is also a jigsaw puzzle,
Showing just as much how very well
All the strange parts fit together.

Which way we look at the drawing
Makes all the difference.
We seem to live in a world of maps:

But in truth we live in a world made
Not of paper and ink but of people.
Those lines are our lives. Together,

Let us turn the map until we see clearly:
The border is what joins us,
Not what separates us.

UNDER THE INFLUENCE OF CELERY

William Pitt Root

Snack-ravenous and sick of sweets, I come to you, at last,
at the bottom of the icebox,
nuzzled by a litter of spilled cherry tomatoes.

Bundle of ionic Mothers puzzled
and chilled by such unlikely progeny,
how wisely my ten sandalled toes point you out
even as my unruly eyes explore smoked meats,
cheeses, and my conscience recites
its prim litany of carcinogens
I've loved all these years
bringing me to you just as I am—
a supplicant as naked in sandals
as the Sonoran sky is
    blue after rain,
 kneeling till my knees ache
    in front of the open fridge
 before the scales fall from my eyes
 and I reach for you, fibrous and delicious.

*

And now I must apologize for such careless poetry.
I see you are not mothers.
                If anything

you are clustered sisters
whose presence evokes a Greek temple haunted
by sacred freshness.

You belong upright, like this, parallel and columnar,
green curls loosely dangling
while your very stillness penetrates
                    to the heart of dance,
a frieze your vegetable scholars surely recognize.

I pull one of you free and immediately
relish the pale curve of
the long inner thigh made straight
by an irresistible pull from the sun,
                    your verdant brilliance
drawn from terrestrial darkness by astral fire!

*

I think of my love, visiting her sisters
in a place far from here,
then of my daughter, learning love this summer
in a place just as distant,
and I try to consider just how it is
we humans keep bringing such fire into our eyes
from the night of the loins and belly
despite the regular flights of eagle-eyed Doubt

and the cancre it tends in the best-lit heart.

*

Seeing it all so clearly
under the influence
of celery,
I am uneasy.
          How

can I ever
eat you, now that you are
lover, daughter,
and I a mere man standing naked,
dumbfounded, not a pretty sight
in the shambles of his kitchen
rummaging for a snack?

*

I eat you because
I am alive
and you
are to be known—not wasted
by wanton sentimentality stalling you
              in the food chain,
preventing your transformation into consciousness.

*

I eat you because
as I love those closest to me
so I love you,
and I would have us all consumed by love.

*

I eat you because I am hungry
and you are food
and sometimes life is this good
and such is the poetry by which we become most ourselves.

ODE TO AMERICA
Sankar Roy

for Langston Hughes

Above your placenta lakes, bald eagle circle
in the celestial light of the newborn stars. Bright-colored
automobiles cross rusty iron bridges
with headlights on through the nightly fog.
Like a procession of monks

chanting a polyphonic growl
of wheel against the dust,
metal against the wind,
humming an astonishing song.

I, too, sing with it,
America! I am your brown son.
See, my skin has the glow of a banana.
My hair is dark as your Iroquois night.
When I am asleep, I shine

like an amethyst pearl. And when the night is still young
in the shrub of wild Iris, across the windowpane,
I chat with Pocahontas!
Daughter of yours, also brown.
She sings while rowing her coffee-colored canoe
through the tribal breeze:

BREATHE

Sometimes I go about pitying myself,
and all the time, I am carried on
great winds across the sky.

We share folklore, you know.
I imitate the voice of my dead grandma:

Rama and Sita leave the kingdom
for fourteen long years to live in a dense forest.
Nowadays they live in a thatched hut home
beside a lotus pond where the moon shines
through the frayed banana leaves.

When Rama goes out gathering
fallen fruits and dead twigs,
a rhombus-eyed deer with golden fur
mesmerizes her from the woods.

No longer can Sita concentrate on her daily chores.
She cannot cook; she cannot take a bath.
The wild dark eyes, untamed but cautious,
follow her even in the dream:

I fly in an amber chariot with my captor.
My dark hair flies through the dark clouds.
A firebird chases us from behind.
For reasons unknown, I like this ride...

Before I could finish my story, Pocahontas was gone,
far away in her canoe of aspen bark, creating waves
in the wind, still swelling like ocean tides

and underneath, our immigrant homes, fragile trees
of the city park shimmer in the blue light
of the frozen moon, as if they were sea weeds.

After the moon is also asleep,
I walk out into the street, aglow
in the starry American light:

Under the neon scissors in the display window
of Harry's Barber Shop, a sign flashes:
                    Walk-ins welcome

Bouquets of dying chrysanthemums displayed
on the shelf of Mary's Flowers:
                    Buy one get one free

White chunks of chicken meat on the illuminated dish
of Moo-Goo-Gai-Pan in Hunan Buffet:
                    Simply the best in town

Grimace of unsold newspaper in the newsstand:
                    Body of Missing Girl Found

Rooster-looking boys with pierced tongues
and chests full of tattoos yell at me from a stolen vehicle:
                    Paki, Paki

Through the unclean panel
of the Fine Oriental Store,
I see a beautiful Chinese man
cleaning the carcass of a pig in the yellow light.
Loins to the left, ribs to the right, shanks in a bag.

And his lover, a stocky man picking eggplants
from the wicker bin
with the attentiveness of Li Po.

I know him better—

once I helped him fill out a form:

Do you show your allegiance to America? YES
Were you ever a Nazi? NO
Do you speak English? YES.
Have you ever been convicted of a crime? NO

I think of my grandpa.
He fought against the Queen's army
one hundred and fifty years after
America fought them at Gettysburg.

Grandpa walked two hundred miles barefoot
following a half-naked man
called Gandhi. In that insane struggle,
they used no guns. I watch him in my musings:

A long procession of men and women,
emaciated, unshaven ragamuffins,
barefoot maidens striding
along a dusty road, chanting—

karenge ya marenge—do or die,

Jasmine blossoms from the lip of a shiny English gun,
coconut leaves shiver in the grunt of the royal bugle,—
scarlet hibiscus blossoms on their banians and saris,
before grandpa falls onto the ground singing,

Raghupati Raghava Raja Ram,   Patita Pavana Sita Ram.

GOAT

C.J. Sage

Hoofed culler of things ignored,
pointy-bearded opportunist,
bedroom-eyed, steel-jawed hoverer on land,

you charm and chump
with your yellow iris, remorselessness
unflinching as a pitchfork among hay,

bailing piles upon piles over a shoulder.
There's a feast wherever you forage.
No lawn for long wherever you live,

you are blamed for lack, the cause of all corrosion.
We leave our gardens unattended, our backs
to both your province and your teeth,

our pant legs at your feet.
The bulk of you is not your horns;
your sum is in your hunger.

ALTAR WHERE I WATCH YOU SLEEP

Dixie Salazar

"The sacred space of an altar encloses
symbolic objects in a designated frame."
—Kay Turner

Your breath moves like liquid sound
searching for a home
a new shore to lap against
So much movement forward
and back, a shifting
border that sets the room afire
kindles the memory
of tongueless shoes, coffee grounds
and smoke alarms
all fresh with promise
but no velocity
Quiet as zip codes smeared
in the rain
quiet as a picture of a window
framed like a window
Quiet as a blue-green fish
content to dock in oxidized dreams,
your breath rises
to the surface
where knotholes and jazz quiver
like stars and whisper
to the buoys... telling them
to never hold still

but still hold
to rumble and glow
like a fixed point
in the speeding constellation
of the sea searching
for a home.

FLORIDA

Adrian Sângeorzan

When we grow old
We'll retire to Florida.
At first we'll send our spirits there
On short holidays
In search of youth without aging
And life without death.

We are a generation with strong and white bones.
We invented hurricanes, globalization and salt water
That we will pass on
To our children or to some foundations
Which will love us with moderation.
The hot sand and the sun will remind us of
The 60s, feminism and the sexual revolution
When the spoiled hormones of communism
Swarmed under our skin giving us true sensations
Which our mothers, unaware
Greased up with butter
On our bread.

Today everything in America is big
The towers, the beaches, people's bellies
The toilets seats

The ideas working on steroids.
Only the spirits still play in the sand
With golden pickaxes.

This is the place for the great retreat.
The last survivors
Cured of all of life's melanoma
Quietly play bridge at the edge of the world.
Their nephews listen to hip-hop on iPods.
We are all so digitalized.
Seagulls blinded by cataract perch
On Poseidon's back
Whose only remains is a floating shoulder blade
And the name of a casino.

We are the next elephants
We'll slowly migrate to Miami
Through the slippery funnel of America.
We still make love without Viagra
Right on the coils of the old watches
Which we'll wind up.
They'll continue to tick under our king size beds
Like a Chinese perpetuum mobile.

On the beach the sand
Escaped from hourglasses
Will build solid castles
Where all the world's languages will be spoken
From which we'll choose for our ears
Some gorgeous coral idioms.

During our last years
We will tan well all over
We will cremate ourselves unnoticeably
More beautiful than Tutankhamen.

SUMMER IS HERE

John Savoie

*"When the branch grows tender and shoots
forth leaves, you know that summer is near."*
—Matthew 24:32

In the stillness of summer's first day
my eyes caught the sheerest puff
of light teasing at the threshold
of vision, a little nimbus coasting
slowly as a sail on the horizon.

At last I had to let it go,
or lose my vision with it, but soon
I spied another, then another,
(my eyes having learned to see in the light)
each drawn along its own destined line.

The furrowed limbs of the cottonwood
arching so high, I could believe
I stood in lee of the tree of life
and these seeds were souls in flight,
coming or going, I couldn't tell.

Till I felt the gust of heat, heard it
rifling through the heart-shaped leaves,
and all at once the air exploded
as when the stars that measure the mind
of God fall from their places—

countless seeds swarmed and scattered,
frenzied as a broken hive,
and spangling leaves, pinned in their places,
roared in harsh saw-toothed sibilance,
Kosovo, Kosovo, Kosovo.

AN ODE TO VIRGINIA TECH, BLACKSBURG, April 16, 2007
Vivian Shipley

"Mockingbirds don't do one thing but make music."
—Harper Lee

The Monday after Thanksgiving was a school holiday,
unleashing us to hunt with our fathers for the first day

of deer season and soak plaid shirts with entrails of a buck.
In Lejunior, Kentucky, after mopping off coal dust, we ate

at kitchen tables stained with blood from squirrel meat
chopped up for burgoo. Disney's Swamp Fox, each January

I killed a squirrel for the tail to sew onto my cap. Hell bent
on fun, cruelty was as irrelevant as lightning bugs I smeared

to make fences phosphorescent. Summer, copperheads came
from woods to sun on blacktop. Mothers came running.

One pitchforked the body while another hoed off the head.
As if pardoning sinners, our neighbor bagged long ones

in burlap in case the spirit moved her husband to take up
serpents at Pentecostal Church of God. Going to the dump

at dusk with an air rifle, I never blew away rats but if a pellet
hit an empty can, a possum would jump, metal armoring

its nose. My aim was better with a Wrist Rocket. Ball bearings
or a stone worked the best. Coke from roadside gravel was light

as cork, too porous to hurt anything. Take aim, then pull back
surgical tubing and the leather pouch became a catapult. Never

stopping to think what I did could not be undone, I targeted
the red breast of a robin which had lured me with its music.

Remembering the silence, bird wings spread into a cross
on the ground, how can I wonder now why Seung-Hui Cho

could harm the blameless, those he didn't know, pull a trigger
again, again until he had silenced thirty-two lives in midsong?

SHOPPING URBAN

Jane Shore

Flip-flopped, noosed in puka beads, my daughter
breezes through the store from headband to toe ring,
shooing me away from the bongs,
lace thongs, and studded dog collars.
And I don't want to see her in that black muscle tee
with SLUT stamped in gold glitter
shrink-wrapped over her breasts,
or those brown and chartreuse retro-plaid
hip-huggers ripped at the crotch.

There's not a shopper here a day over twenty
except me and another mother
parked in chairs at the dressing room entrance
beyond which we are forbidden to go.
We're human clothes racks.
Our daughters have trained us
to tamp down the least flicker of enthusiasm
for the nice dress with room to grow into,
an item they regard with sullen, nauseated,
eyeball-rolling disdain.

Waiting in the line for a dressing room,
my daughter checks her cleavage.
Her bellybutton's a Cyclops eye
peeking at other girls' armloads of clothes.

What if she's missed something—
that faux leopard hoodie? those coffee-wash flares?
Sinking under her stash of blouses,
she's a Shiva of tangled sleeves.

And where did she dig up that new tie-dyed
tank top I threw away in '69,
and the purple wash 'n' wear psychedelic dress
I washed and wore
and lost on my Grand Tour of Europe,
and my retired hippie Peace necklace
now recycled, revived, re-hip?

I thought they were gone—
like the tutus and tiaras and wands
when she morphed from ballerina
to fairy princess to mermaid to tomboy,
refusing to wear dresses ever again.
Gone, those pastel party dresses,
the sleeves, puffed water wings buoying her up
as she swam into waters over her head.

THE NEW TREATY
Barry Silesky

after Laima Simanavichus, painting on plexiglass

As if the white pool above the layers
of rose, white, then crimson sediment
erupted: a slow birth on a planet
we never knew, spilling
the soup of muted primaries over

the second-hand furniture, the rooftops
the pigeons stalk against the vacant sky.
How long we've wanted to taste it,
to board the ship that will take us,
painted next to the window. We can hear

shouts coming closer, glass
shatter in the street below. We turn up
the music, trade the jerusalem cherry
the insects gnawed all year for a Swedish ivy,
as if to confirm the tickets, prepare

the ship's departure. With interest rates
down, a whole new neighborhood opens
its lawns—brown and gritty as the old,
but a fine place to deposit
the children we want to exist, the woman

across the courtyard, who's screaming
at them again. The days' headlines will look
so colorful in their new surroundings,

delivering happy memories of the peeling
wallpaper, the gouged door we left.

We can give the cat to the landlord,
and we're sad to leave, but
the excitement is irresistible—
the city's parade marches into
the living room, and so many restaurants

send their invitations we won't even notice
the wildlife chewing on the basement timbers,
the latest explosion
lighting up the back porch
with a terrific view of the old tracks.
Finally, our own parking space;
and when the train shakes the bed, we'll haul out
the old records and sing along all night,
drowning the riot with those great oldies
our ship sails on while we figure out who to blame.

Odd then, not to have seen the woman
from the first. She's been pushing
into the streets all these years, arms swelling
the shirt in the latest fashion.
                              But the oversight's
passé, another symptom of the disease we keep thinking
is cured—the musty clubroom virus, the stench
of cigar cleaned out
                    like old newpaper. Except
they keep collecting in the closets, spreading
their old news. When I meet her
I try to rely on the forms
                          of polite conversation
I've learned for such occasions, but they give me
away again, pointing out what I can't
see:

        the face behind the white pool
in the picture; the reason it's dressed in such colors
to catch my attention and push away
the real work collecting.

                    *

These views keep seducing us, never explaining
            their presence—the v-neckline floating
behind a layer of cloud, a bare suggestion:
            is she coming? Will her face deliver
the promise the slender arms wrap in these colors?

Then stretched across the bottom in solid red,
            another perspective, but cut off
past the hips and shoulders: naked, flushed
            beyond the possible, the slight dip tracing her
back, the curved line at the edge, her breast . . .

Does it always come to sex, then?
            An important diversion, and it does have a way
of spreading into the day, absorbing the rotten
            weather; compensation for this
confusion, at least until

it dissipates into the usual bills and paper
            piled on the table, the phone
about to ring—
            We can hardly afford the indulgence,
but denying that pleasure is just as risky—

                    *

One more step away from the flesh riding us
into the exhibitions that might

instruct us through the afternoon. That room's so vast,
so many aisles spinning

                                  their intricate patterns,
it's too easy to get lost, and the old etiquette's
no help. Those instructions are another myth,
hopelessly outdated as the originals:

                          walk around
the fire pit chanting and see what happens.
For some the ritual's a way to live forever,
or at least until the war

                              finds us. Still, you have to
believe, and such faith isn't a ring
at the local jeweler's, a painting framed and ready
to choose. Instead, it simply

                                 happens—not an
accident,
exactly, but you study the map, tear up
the sidewalk, and if you're lucky, in the right place
and time, a handful of the right pills, or money, or charm,
 a particular conversation with, say

           *

that woman—what other reason to go on this way?
      Soon enough the day will be gone
completely, the war continuing its latest arrangement
      as we negotiate the treaty over coffee: if she'll just
do the laundry once in a while, I'll fix supper, etc. . . .

She demurs—there's work to be done,
      appointments downtown, catalogues
of the current literature to sort through. We don't
      really believe in those chants,
but today we'll try anything.

WHEAT

Warren Slesinger

for Jim Coleman

Out of town, you pull off the road
at a wayside with a clear view of the county:
square-topped fields of high-yield wheat
that once were rock-ribbed hills;

sunlight blocks of silence without a house
or barn on land that seems too large to farm,
save for the machinery that crosses it in tandem:
the air glimmering with ground-up dust

when an International Harvester turns
with a surge of its engine, and the blades
take it in the opposite direction while the hills
absorb the sunlight as the machinery

moves downwind, and the silence
of the former woods and forgotten streams
settles in again on poles and power lines

along the road for mile after mile,
and still the distance to another range
of nameless streams and hills.

LATE CENTURY ODE FOR THE COMMON DEAD

Arthur Smith

1.
Not history, not the past—
I see that now—
Students on a commons stage,
Crowded and crowding back
Red-faced with bullhorns,
The San Francisco
Bay winds whipped
Colder by helicopters crossing
And re-crossing the square,
Each pendulum-like pass
Lower than the one before
And louder, a wake rolling over
Those of us stopped on
The way elsewhere,
Trying to make out
Between turbulences what was
Being said.

I'm still trying to make it out
Twenty-five years later
In Knoxville where I live,
On the campus where I work,
On the lower south side of a hill
Falling off to the Tennessee,
Just uphill

From a chestnut oak
I'm standing below.
Here, in 1901, breaking ground
For a women's hall long since lived-in
And outlived
And razed back to the ground
It seemed to spring from,
The bodies of eight soldiers, all Union, men and boys,
      were unearthed—
A few buttons, bones,
Uniform tatters.

Now, what with the blizzard
And flooding, the dogwoods are late lifting
Their broken cups
To the sunlight working
April's inclination, the same light
Fostering the thickets after Chickamauga
And leading the buttercups there in their slow yellow
      fan across the meadows.

To my right, a van
Idling in front of
The nuclear engineering complex,
And traffic on the bridge south,
And a tugboat's vented blast,
And behind me, the stadium,
Its pillars and girders
Weathering without sound,
As the library on my left is,
Its stories terraced,
Receding in shadows,
And in front of me, topping the hill,
The tower of the oldest building from which, now,
The cracking of a window

Going up,
A man in a white shirt
Leaning out, looking around.

2.
Once, not far from here,
Was a graveyard no one's heard of,
One of several in Dempsey Branch,
Just south of Mt. Gay
In far southwestern West Virginia.

From anywhere in it, a thrown rock
Would clear the chicken wire
Fencing in the stones
That barely last past the names—
Ballard Ellis, his wife Bessie,
Their children Clifford and Lura Belle
And Roy Lee, aged two months,
The lettering netted over
With vines, more and more difficult
To read.

The graveyard's known
As Mounts,
After the grocer
Who gave the land around the time
The killings ended farther south
Between the Hatfields and McCoys,
And just before they started up
Among the union organizers,
And the Pinkertons,
And those fierce plain folks
The coalminers
Of neighboring Matewan.

I know these things because the Ellises—
My mother's family—were buried there,
As Mounts was, until last fall
When the road from Holden
To Logan went in
And my mother's youngest sister
Witnessed the exhumation of the bodies—
What passed for them—
The remains trucked
Twenty miles
To Forest Lawn Cemetery
Near Chapmanville:

Of their father,
A blue tie, she swears—
No bones, nothing
Of his coffin; of the mother,
On one of several
Fingerbones, a wedding band.

It sounds apocryphal, but
I've stood there and
Thrown a rock
Clear of it,
Out into the underbrush,
And I've seen what had been given
Taken back.

When I look at the white fog
Pooling in the valleys
And the cloud-rivers
Winding thinly
Between the pitched hills,
I begin to hear from the pines

That breathing I thought of
Once as mournful, and then
As the one sound desire
Underscores the others with, and finally
As wind in the needles,
Bearing nothing,
And bearing it away.

3.
We talk about the end of the world
As though it were the end
Of the world.
We like to think
The time and place we occupy
Is central.

It is nothing to the markers
Lining the narrow circular drive
Of National Cemetery,
The headstones
Wheeling as I stop
And walk to the nearest—
Dead so long
I run my hand over the smooth-
Looking stones—
They're deeply pitted
And coarse, not comforting—
They're not supposed to be comforting,
These graves,
Men and women of whom
Nothing's known, other than
Names as common
As those I hear and say
Almost every day—
Hodges and Ayres, Holt and McClung,

BREATHE

Neyland and Morgan and Stokely—
On towers and stadiums,
On libraries:

Teachers' names and merchants'
And soldiers' more widely remembered,
Perhaps, than these,
But all challenged in the dailiness
Of their own beliefs, with few of them
Comforted by the pasts
They looked back to,
And none of them rescued by what was
Already known,
Though they brought what they knew as far forward
As they could
Before it became
Part of the story
Time now tells about them.

Wherever the eight are,
I can't find them.
Neither can the caretaker
Scanning the tops, wave and wave.

It's late July
As I walk back to the car,
Sweating in a drought summer,
The walnut trees bearing up,
The lawn not,
The maple leaves
Browning from the tips,
The shade afforded by them
Sweeping the day's heat along,
The headstones cooling
On either side in row on row rippling

From the center, the plots
Lettered and numbered—
D 103, 102, 101—
The names on the other side,
Cut into and
Weathering back out of time:

Wm Winn, Tenn Inf,

And Robt Laferty, US Hv Arty,

And John Davis of North Carolina,

And Wm Allen, and so on.

LAST BLUE

Gerald Stern

You want to get the color blue right,
just drink some blue milk from a blue cup;
wait for the blue light of morning
or evening with its blue aftermath.

You want to understand,
look at the parking lines outside my window,
the neon moon outside Jabberwocky's.

And funk! You have to know funk.
a touch of blue at the base of the spine;
long threads going into your heart;
a streaming fountain you pour into your own bowl.

My dead sister's eyes!
Those her porcelain twin at the Lambertville Flea,
twenty dollars a day for the small table,
all the merde you need to get you across the river.

And one kind of blue for a robin's egg;
and one kind of blue for a bottle of ink.
Two minds to fathom the difference.

Your earrings which as far as I can see
are there as much to play with as to look at.
Your blue pencil
which makes your eyes Egyptian. Blue bells, bluebirds,

from Austin, Texas, the dead huckster
who drank potassium, Governor Bush
who drank milk of magnesia; a chorus of saints
from Wylie Avenue and one kind of blue

for my first prayer shawl and one kind of blue for the robe
Fra Lippo gave to Mary. Blue from Mexico
and blue from Greece, that's where the difference lay
between them, in the blues; a roomful of scholars,

in Montreal one year, in New York another,
that is blue, blue was their speech, blue
were their male and female neckties, their food was blue,
their cars were rented, Christmas lights

were in the lobby, one of the bars and peanuts
in all the urns and on the upper floors
the hospitality rooms were crowded with livid
sapphire cobalt faces—I was blue

going into the tunnel, I am blue every night
at three or four o'clock; our herring was blue,
we ate it with Russian rye and boiled potatoes,
and in the summer fresh tomatoes, and coffee

mixed with sugar and milk; I sat in a chair
so close to Sonny Terry I could hear
him mumble, the criticism he made
of his own sorrow, but I was that close to Pablo

BREATHE

Casals in 1950, talk about blue, and
though I left it a thousand times I stood—
since I didn't have a seat—in front of an open
window of Beth Israel in Philadelphia

to hear the sobbing, such a voice, a dog
came up to me that night out of the blue
and put his muzzle in my hand nor would he
leave me for a minute, he would have stayed

with me forever and followed me up to my house
which butted onto the woods in back of the synagogue
and sat outside my door; or blue on the street
outside a Parlour near the Port Authority—

my seed inside—or blue in Ocean Grove
where sky and sea combined and walking the boardwalk
into the wind and blue in a shrink's small parking lot
watching the clock and blue in my mother's arms

always comforting her and blue with my daughter
starving herself and blue with my wife all day
playing solitaire or drawing houses and blue,
though smiling, when I came into the world, they called me

Jess Willard, thirteen pounds, and I had just hammered
Jack Dempsey into the ropes and I was shouting—
in a tinny voice—it sounded like someone weeping—
it always sounded like that—everything living.

THE FRUITED PLAIN
Maria Terrone

At a Korean Greengrocer's,
Jackson Heights, Queens, NYC

The purple mountains are so high,
our hands must climb to reach
the top, the plum at its peak
of perfection. Once there, we strive

for more. No surprise—desire is why we came,
and this fruited plain knows no fence,
pushing out to sidewalk shoppers intent
on seizing the best. We sniff, squeeze, exclaim

to companions in Farsi, French, English, Urdu,
Spanish, Cantonese, Korean, Russian, Creole.
By the cash register, a sign extols:
We Will Never Forget. Citrus wear the tattoos

of corporations. Aztec-faced men build pyramid
displays, unpack papayas, their arms branded
with hearts and names of loved ones stranded
south of desert borders. At ten p.m., they sweep up fetid

remains, vanishing into a back room
with plastic buckets of unsold bouquets.
At eight, Kim and her brother, Sam, raise the steel gate
again on amber waves of ginger, bins stacked

with aloe huge as oars, tofu squares afloat. Kim knows
how plants can keep her customers well or steer
them back to health—the Irish supers; women who peer
from burkas; spike-heeled retirees; Croatian

carpenters; turbaned Sikhs with flag pins
on their suits. Proud to Be American from sea
to shining sea of blueberries, blood oranges, kiwi,
yams, yucca, mangoes, guava, pumpkins

that teachers at P.S. 69 will buy and soon carve
for the children, their grinning faces also lit
from within. They'll dress like goblins, learn the Holy Writ:
United We Stand. This is America. No one starves.

HEALING IN THE LANGUAGE OF TREES
Pamela Uschuk

The day she could walk again
she retrieved stampeding leaves,
which in the language of trees
are hearts, and she pressed
them into her scars.
For weeks, it had been leaves
and high tension wires, all she could see
from her paralyzed view as she lay
in the back of her husband's van
that shuttled her from office
to doctor's office
and home. The electric wires
were incisions that bisected sky
and dismembered flying birds.
Only the leaves slam-danced
in the arms of the wind
as she danced wild
in arms that called themselves love or lust.
Leaves were daily medicine
transfused directly into her veins,
leaves crackling like the burning souls
of butterflies, despite
the world cracking up around her, despite
thousands of troops

sent to the Middle East
or the grave father's face
of the President with the crooked grin.
Even when she watched TV
on her stomach, she could see
he spoke out of the side of his mouth.
Leaves gave up their green
to gold, going to flame
red as desire. Leaves suspended her
above the labyrinth of despair.
Leaves and her body healing
itself, rewording gravity's verdict
for her constant bending to mop floors
or picking up after her untidy husband
or lifting boxes to move
from rented house to house.
So the day she began to walk again
even if it was with jaded gait,
it was leaves she cradled
like a lover's face, leaves—
maple, ash, oak, tulip tree,
sumac, hawthorne, hickory—leaves
to carry her into the sky
away from exploding trains
and car bombs half a world away.
Leaves were silk slicking her skin,
lover tongues inventing her name in the sweet
patois of trees, heart after heart
after heart. They were all she needed
now that she began to samba
against destruction and its lies.

ST. CATHERINE OF SIENA'S DAY

Wendy Vardaman

Fifty daffodils, one hundred
hyacinths—buried
last fall produce
only a handful of halfway resurrections:
limp wings on weak
necks emerging from a cracked
tomb—the wrong
soil and a long
winter of low
temperatures without insulating snow.

Content yourself with this:
a few lines, less
than you conceived
by the time they arrived—
scribbled on the back of something else; almost forgotten
between their thought and the interruption
of children, practice,
questions of dinner and the day, cookies
for tomorrow, the last
batch
burned inedible—
and their retrieval;

or with dandelions—too many
to count—bright as any
daffodil but longer lasting, cheerful,
less temperamental,
and a neighbor's sign: Free
Daylilies, already
tall, fresh dug, ready to return
to bad soil like saints to heaven.

PREACHING FOR WINOS
Jon Veinberg

For you, who have grown tired of stumbling
through doorways, counting sighs and holding on to air,
for you, whose years have passed quickly
and whose hours stand still, who wait for tomorrow
to wash out the fumes and sewer stink of the shirt
you slept in; I will tie the shoe no one would claim.

I will shadow your soul as you tiptoe
past the guard dogs roaming the used car lots,
and the store clerks scrubbing death is forever
graffiti off their windows and the bail jumper shuffling
his losses, past the paramedics making their rounds
and the children in bowed apartment buildings

popping their knuckles, scavenging for razor blades
and flattening pennies into quarters on railroad tracks.
For you, whose hallways I have loitered,
whose libraries I have chewed my wrists in, whose wall
I have leaned my fists against to fight sleep
because in my dreams there were no oceans,

no angel to slide the rent through the wind-sawed door.
The gardens of childhood went to seed,
white-lighting out of kilter down the alley

and through the night under the neon's cruel wink,
beneath the smell of bacon grease floating
from the projects and the loan shark trimming his nails

on the star-blocked fire escape, the flies in frenzy,
and the luckless streetwalker staring into the mist
of headlights and dead nights, and the bookmaker
working overtime, and the crack house keeping its light on
for fresh runaways who dream for a world to behold
other than this one. For you, who are destined to die

at bus stops hugging your knees and blowing on your hands,
for you, who have asked for forgiveness
and gotten 7-day lockdowns and bitten ears in fights
over stolen batteries and cheap rides,
I will dance on my knees to save you. I will place my hand
in yours. It will be a collision of flesh. Hell will close its eye

if you listen as I coax fire back into your dead eyes.
For you, they have boarded up the health clinics
and invented deadbolts for confessionals and food banks,
for you, I have brought oranges and an umbrella
to draw out the hunger you were born into. I am here
to make your suffering matter. I am here to rewrite your epitaph.

JAPANESE GARDEN
Benjamin Vogt

Enter through the hedge like wind slipping from itself a stained earthly veil. Step forward with calm to find a stone in your path—all flowers open slow. Beside the tea garden rinse your hands and mouth to show you walk from rivers. Speak softly in shade, smell cool dew against your feet, hear nothing but light. Yatsuhashi leads across calm water, trains stars beneath the surface. Beside a black pine one stone looks up, one over; something speaks inside. Waves of sand move still around three green islands, yet mountains cry within. Weeping willows trace the arc of my back like clouds—one leaf trembles. Lotus in the pond; we must rest here awhile like wonted stones. As the sky, gravel; as rivers, flesh of peony; without me, you.

ODE TO MY HANDS
Diane Wakoski

"Beauty is momentary in the mind—
The fitful tracing of a portal;
But in the flesh it is immortal."
—Wallace Stevens from "Peter Quince at the Clavier"

Sometimes I think my old
hands are beautiful
like Arabians nuzzled into Kentucky bluegrass,
their coats with the satin of chestnuts before they
are roasted. My hands, though,
are spotted, more like giraffe skin,
and lying across my book,
as if they might be
newborn, awkward foals,
not able to be deft with small pieces,
like the backs of my pearl earring studs.
Babies, looking up but resting
against their mother book.

My handwriting gets smaller and
harder to read. These spotted translucent hands seem
too plump to write a thin line. They
do look like miniature hens,
pale frogs, or shaky-legged colts
as they rest on pages of Wallace Stevens or
on my denim knees—still they cleave
to my body, though it hardly seems to belong
to me any more. My mind curls also,
like the giraffe's lashes,

fringed petal-like and so inappropriately, as if
for Romance, as do my old hands.

In T'ai Chi, you are supposed to hold out
"beautiful lady wrists," and as I was circling through the form
this morning, piercing into my living room windows came
a shaft of light that exactly passed into my undulating
hands, a pen of light dipped into its own ink, and I
pulled it through the air, knowing for a moment that despite my age,
I still could reinvent myself, perhaps even still write this ode
with the hands
that have always longed to play at
Peter Quince's clavier.

ODE TO THE FIVE AND DIME
Suellen Wedmore

A kid could go to Woolworth's
  all by herself, pocket jingling
    with a few coins, and buy a mood ring,
      crayons, coloring book,

Orphan Annie paper dolls,
  and still have enough left over
    to sip a chocolate ice-cream soda
      at the marble-topped counter

in the back of the store,
  listening all the while
    to the rain-forest warble
      of parakeet and canary,

and she might imagine—
  if she could talk Mom
    into a raise in her allowance—
      she could bring home

one of those jungle songsters
  in a green wire cage.
    You could go to Woolworth's
      if Mom was working afternoons,

and ease your loneliness with a hot dog
  or macaroni and cheese,

and the waitress bustling toward you
  in an apron stained with ketchup

might say, How's things goin', Kiddo?
  On display, you could find
    the perfect mother's day gift
      for just 89 cents—perfume

in a bottle the shape of a heart,
  angel, or violin, beribboned
    and artfully reflecting
      those incandescent bulbs

dangling on black wires
  from an embossed metal ceiling.
    My friend Mary Catherine and I
      spent hours hovering near the counter

where tubes of lipstick were lined up
  in shiny rows, thankful for
    the clerk in blue-tinted hair,
      who left us alone to discover

what color fuchsia cornflower
  really was. There were rows
    of satin ribbon, buttons, snaps,
      zippers, hooks and eyes;

how can we hold ourselves together
  now that the five and dime is gone?
    I tested a dozen bolts of cloth
      for softness, before I bought

a quarter yard of calico
  to dress Betsy McCall.

There were fountain pens with pink
and turquoise ink, and paper

edged in gold for that letter
to a special pen pal. A plastic
tow truck with real rubber tires
could make a boy's whole week—

whatever you dreamed,
it was there, though perhaps
you didn't know what you needed
until you saw it bright and new,

calling out to you from just
beyond your reach.
I was never more sure
of my place in the world

than when Grandma gave me
a quarter, told me to buy
myself something special,
at Woolworth's five and dime.

Gary Young

The earth submits to seasonal drift. The stars slide, and the planets swing higher over the horizon every day. This morning the sun sent a shaft of light through a rift in the redwoods; it followed the steep angle of the canyon, skirted the stream, the wild azalea, the granite cut bank, and shined on the brick stoop beneath the stone arch at our gate. It rested there only for a moment, but my son found it. He sat there warming himself, and anyone watching the light play over his body could have believed he was made of gold.

Biographies and Commentaries:

Kim Addonizio lives in Oakland, CA. Her most recent book of poems is *What Is This Thing Called Love* (Norton, 2005). In 2009, Norton will be publishing *Ordinary Genius: A Guide for the Poet Within*, and a new collection, *Lucifer at the Starlite*.

Addonizio writes: "I was inspired to write an ode after reading several by Dean Young. I was also finishing up my next collection and thought writing an ode might be a way to lighten some of the darkness in the book—why not find something to praise? Of course, I couldn't help the darkness creeping in, but I hope in the end that 'God Ode' does, as Adam Zagajewski wrote, 'try to praise the mutilated world.'"

Dick Allen's most recent collection is *Present Vanishing: Poems*, published in 2008 by Sarabande Books, as were his two earlier volumes, *The Day Before: New Poems* and *Ode to the Cold War: Poems New and Selected*. He taught most recently at the West Chester Poetry Conference in 2007, and is the Charles A. Dana Professor of Literature Emeritus at the University of Bridgeport, in Connecticut, from which he took early retirement. Allen has received a Pushcart Prize, and Poetry Writing Fellowships from the N.E.A. and Ingram Merrill Foundations, among numerous other national awards.

Allen writes: "'Quiet, Quiet Now' is a paean to America, and one of the results of a commission from a national bicentennial project, as well as of the annual 10,000 mile driving trips my wife and I make around the nation each year. The sense of calm waits everywhere in our country, once one gets beyond the terror of our cities and our nervous obsessions. We've found this sense always quite lovely, always waiting to receive us—a sense the poem tries to evoke by especially using parallelism rhythms and tactile imagery."

Ralph Angel is the author of four books of poetry: *Exceptions and Melancholies: Poems 1986-2006* (2007 PEN USA Poetry Award); *Twice Removed*; *Neither World*, (James Laughlin Award of The Academy of American Poets); and *Anxious Latitudes*; as well as a translation of

Federico García Lorca's *Poema del cante jondo / Poem of the Deep Song*. Other awards include a gift from the Elgin Cox Trust, a Pushcart Prize, a Gertrude Stein Award, the Willis Barnstone Poetry Translation Prize, a Fulbright Foundation fellowship and the Bess Hokin Award of the Modern Poetry Association. Mr. Angel is Edith R. White Distinguished Professor of English and Creative Writing at the University of Redlands, and a member of the M.F.A. Program in Writing faculty at Vermont College of Fine Arts. Originally from Seattle, he lives in Los Angeles.

Angel writes: "I don't much remember making this poem, though I'd been listening to John Coltrane's 'A Love Supreme' over and over again for a number of days. The poem's not about Coltrane, or his extraordinary composition, 'A Love Supreme,' but the title is the title of its first movement. And, I'm sure, in some inexplicable way, communes with one of my many gods, John Coltrane."

James Arthur's poems have appeared or are forthcoming in *The New Yorker, The New Republic, The Nation,* and *The Southern Review.* He is currently a Stegner Fellow in Poetry at Stanford University and was the 2006-2007 Amy Lowell Travelling Poetry Scholar. He lives in Oakland with his wife, the writer Shannon Robinson.

Arthur writes: "I took the epigraph for this poem from *Triggering Town,* Richard Hugo's wonderful guide for young poets. Although Hugo's comment about semicolons is playful, he is also making a serious point: that semicolons parse out and clarify logical relationships, whereas the analogies and correspondences of poetic reasoning are often surprising, or even ambiguous. On the other hand, one of the pleasures of poetry, at least for me, is that it allows the intellect to wrestle with intuitions and with the dilemmas of the heart. That's what I see in this poem—a wish for longings to have definite endings and beginnings, and for there to be a grammar of existence that helps us make sense of what we feel."

Sally Ashton of Los Gatos, CA, is author of the collection, *These Metallic Days* from Main Street Rag. Her poetry and reviews have recently appeared or are forthcoming in *Sentence: a journal of prose poetics, Poet Lore, Mississippi Review, Dos Passos Review,* and *failbetter.com.* She teaches at San Jose State University and through various workshops and retreats.

She is editor of the *DMQ Review*.

Ashton writes: "This poem traces a route I've traveled since childhood, through a landscape that is changing yet remains much the same as it was years ago. What has changed can still be recovered through memory and imagination, even through this recitation. An ode calls attention to something deserving notice. It seeks to recognize what is worthy."

David Baker lives in Granville, Ohio, and teaches at Denison University and in the M.F.A. program for writers at Warren Wilson College. He also serves as Poetry Editor of *The Kenyon Review*. His ninth book of poems, *Never-Ending Birds*, will appear in 2009 from Norton.

Baker writes: "The ode is the odd lyric mode of the classical varieties. More public, less intimate, more social, less meditative, its rhetoric tends to be heightened, even hortatory. This is thorny for contemporary poets, for the ode can easily veer into propaganda or melodrama. To help me with these poems, I turned in 'To Winter' to the great odist John Keats; and in 'Midwest Ode' I interfused the elegiac with the odic in memory of William Matthews, whose poetry beautifully negotiated the vexed terrain between the public and the private."

Marvin Bell lives in Iowa City, Iowa, and Port Townsend, Washington. His most recent collection of poetry, *Mars Being Red* (Copper Canyon Press, 2007), Bell's nineteenth collection of poems, is definitively wartime. Retired from the Iowa Writers' Workshop, Bell teaches for the brief-residency M.F.A. program based in Oregon at Pacific University. He is responsible for a poetic and philosophic form known as "the dead man poems."

Bell writes: "The ode, traditionally a lyric of exaltation, might now be a catalog of the life force in the context of the human condition. Said another way, it was always about the planet, never about us. In the end, every ode is about energy—its gathering and its dispersion."

Eleanor Berry lives in rural Lyons, Oregon, where she moved in 1994, after growing up in southern New England and then living for 25 years near the Great Lakes. A book of her poems, *Green November*, was published in 2007 by Traprock Books, an independent publisher of poetry based in Eugene, Oregon. Poems of hers have been published in other anthologies and in literary magazines, including *Calyx, Comstock Review, Crab Orchard Review, Hawai'i Pacific Review, Nimrod, Spoon River Poetry Review,* and *Windfall: A Journal of Poetry of Place.* Her essays on poetry have been published in journals and edited collections, most recently, *Reading the Middle Generation Anew* (University of Iowa Press, 2006). She has taught literature and writing at colleges and universities in Milwaukee, Wisconsin, and at Willamette University in Salem, Oregon.

Berry's "Ode in Shades of Green" was inspired by the western Oregon landscape, with its extraordinary multitude of plant species, and by Gerard Manley Hopkins' "Pied Beauty," which has resonated for her since she first read it in eighth grade.

Erin M. Bertram is the author of four chapbooks, most recently *The Urge to Believe Is Stronger than Belief Itself* (Cherry Pie Press, 2008). Her work has appeared or is forthcoming in *Bloom, Copper Nickel, The Laurel Review, So to Speak,* and others. She recently completed an M.F.A., along with a Certificate in Women, Gender, and Sexuality Studies, at Washington University in St. Louis, where she teaches writing. She edits *Shadowbox Press.*

Bertram says: "I'm drawn to odes, as they're one manifestation of gratitude."

Robin Behn lives in Birmingham, Alabama and teaches in the M.F.A. Program at The University of Alabama and for Vermont College of Fine Arts. Her most recent book of poems is *Horizon Note,* from the University of Wisconsin Press.

Behn writes: "I wrote this poem after going back to my hometown of Barrington, Illinois, 38 miles from Chicago. I grew up in a house built in 1860 in this small town surrounded by cornfields. I used to ride my bike out into the country for miles and miles. Now, that land is divided into one acre plots, each with its own McMansion. Surrounding them, the dizzying repetition and fluorescent glower of bigger-is-better retail, what green there is shrunken to token, postage-stamp-sized 'forest preserves,' while names like 'Woodfield' and 'Hawthorn' are assigned to malls. My own attempts at bittersweet song brought to mind Sandburg's ode to Chicago—how, for him, progress was something to praise. Mine is an ironic ode compared to his, but also, I hope, an ode with some singing in it, a song that may be the sum total sound of all the little engines of all the little cars filling up all the big lots..."

Craig Blais was a 2007 recipient of an AWP Intro Award; his work has appeared in *Best New Poets 2007, Bellingham Review, Hayden's Ferry Review*, and *The Pinch*, among other magazines. Currently, he teaches at Sookmyung Women's University in Seoul, South Korea. "Ode to Memory: Self-Portrait with Seven Fingers II" previously appeared in Wichita State's literary magazine, *Mikrokosmos*.

Blais writes: "After attending a Chagall retrospective in Seoul in the summer of 2004, I left the museum hungover, wondering why the work had failed to touch me on the visceral level I knew it should have. Certain the disconnect was in myself and not the work, I set about to reclaim some of the magic and lucidity of my own childhood by entering into an extended dialog with Chagall—employing the same personal, surreal, and whimsical imagery so prevalent in his work. The sequence of poems that ensued led me through the less-traveled corridors of my childhood with Marc Chagall as guide. In this way, I believe the poem to be both an ode to the artist and an ode to memory itself."

Michelle Bitting was born, raised, and lives in Los Angeles, CA. She is thrilled to be the recipient of the inaugural DeNovo First Book Award, and have her book *Good Friday Kiss* (C&R Press, 2008). Her work is forthcoming or published in *Prairie Schooner, Passages North, Narrative, Crab Orchard Review, Rattle*, and others.

Bitting writes: "'Endurance' was inspired by a mentor's many brilliant lyric-narrative pieces, poems that lance the descriptive heart and yet through honesty, big spirit, and an unwavering eye, soar beyond the nitty-gritty truth of this terrible, terribly beautiful world we're hell-o'-lucky to be breathing in."

Bruce Bond's collections of poetry include *Cinder*, *The Throats of Narcissus*, *Radiography*, *The Anteroom of Paradise*, *Independence Days*, and a new volume *Blind Rain*, from LSU Press. His poetry has appeared *in Best American Poetry*, *The Yale Review*, *The Georgia Review*, *The Paris Review*, and many other journals. Presently he is Regents Professor of English at the University of North Texas and Poetry Editor for *American Literary Review*.

Bond writes: "When the first Gulf War hit, I was living in a national park in the middle of Pennsylvania, just outside a small town where I taught at Lock Haven University. This poem grew out of the great confusion of sentiment that surrounded that war, the odd euphoria of the stock market, the euphemistic Desert Storm t-shirts, the alarming distance with which we at home experienced the violence abroad, a kind of video game view of bright blips on screens as our bombs hit their tiny targets. To top it off a heavy snowstorm buried us which made travelling hazardous and heightened both the otherworldly beauty of the place and the sense of alienation that fell from the sky. And as ever the chores of moving ahead in light and in spite of history gone awry."

Laure-Anne Bosselaar is the author of *Small Gods of Grief*, winner of the Isabella Gardner Prize, *The Hour Between Dog and Wolf*, and *A New Hunger*, selected as an ALA Notable Book. She is the editor of four anthologies. The recipient of a Pushcart Prize, she teaches at Sarah Lawrence College and at the Low Residency M.F.A. Program at Pine Manor College.

Bosselar writes: "When I moved to the USA from Belgium, I fell deeply in love with the English language. As this is the fourth language I learned, I wanted to write an ode to English, expressing how some new words 'tasted' as I was learning them."

Earl Braggs, UC Foundation Professor of English, teaches creative writing, poetry, African-American literature, and Russian literature at the UT-Chattanooga. He is the author of five collections of poetry, including *Hat Dancer Blue* (winner of the 1992 Anhinga Prize), *Walking Back From Woodstock*, *House on Fontanka*, *Crossing Tecumseh Street*, *In Which Language Do I Keep Silent: New and Selected Poems*, and he is currently working on a volume entitled *Sketches of Spain*. In addition to his numerous prizes for poetry and fiction, he has been named Outstanding Professor by the Student Government Association, and Outstanding Teacher by The University of Tennessee National Alumni Association. He was recently awarded Individual Artist Grants from Chattanooga Allied Arts and The Tennessee Commission for the Arts.

Braggs writes: "'Miles Plays Trumpet at the Funeral of Malcolm X' is an attempt to see life at the time from the perspective of a newly-converted Muslim prisoner, locked up in prison and locked out of the larger society. It examines what it means to lose (Malcolm's death) the only symbol of hope when despair is not affordable."

Sean Brendan-Brown is a medically-retired Marine currently living in Olympia, Washington. A graduate of the Iowa Writers' Workshop, he received a 1997 N.E.A. poetry fellowship, and has published with the *Notre Dame Review*, *Wisconsin Review*, *The Southampton Review*, *Hunger Magazine*, and the University of Iowa Press anthologies *American Diaspora* and *Like Thunder*.

Brendan-Brown writes: "'A Night So Pure the Love of God Seemed Real' is about an actual night, and I began writing the poem the following afternoon. I remember thinking I was still in a dream: everything was so calm, so clear, so exact in detail, and for that moment I came as close to understanding God as I ever will."

Christopher Buckley's *Modern History* is newly available from Tupelo Press. His sixteenth book of poems, *Rolling the Bones*, is due from EWU Press in fall 2009. He has received two N.E.A. grants, a Fulbright Award in Creative Writing, four Pushcart prizes, and most recently the James Dickey Prize from *Five Points*. For 2007-2008 he was a Guggenheim Fellow in poetry. He teaches in the creative writing department at the University of California-Riverside.

Buckley writes: "If there is another world, another life, then surely the light of this world is the light of that one. Most of my poems—whether dreaming ('Sycamore Canyon Nocturne') or daydreaming ('Dispatch from the Garden at 57')—are looking for that light and hoping to discover and hold some part of transcendence. The poems' projects are to praise and love the world."

Elena Karina Byrne, a graduate of Sarah Lawrence College, is a visual artist, teacher, book reviewer, editor, Poetry Consultant and Moderator for *The Los Angeles Times* Festival of Books, and former 12-year Regional Director of the Poetry Society of America. She is also Literary Programs Director for The Ruskin Art Club and the Poetry Arts teacher for the Idylwild Academy of Arts. Elena's recent publications include, *Best American Poetry 2005, The Yale Review, Paris Review, American Poetry Review, Poetry, Volt, Denver Quarterly, Colorado Review, Virginia Quarterly Review, Ploughshares, Antioch Review, Verse, The Journal, Crazyhorse, Poetry Daily Anthology,* and *Anthology of Magazine Verse & Yearbook of American Poetry.* Books include: *The Flammable Bird* (Zoo Press/Tupelo Press, 2002) and *Masque* (Tupelo Press, 2008).

Byrne writes: "My 'Ode to Rain' was written as a part of a series called, 'The Fables (A Monologue)' in my forthcoming book, *This Fable Language*, and emerged somewhere between the alchemy of word origin and personal mythology. The process unfolded a sensory translation of rain in several guises. The italicized line, 'Once there were two brothers...' belongs to M.F.K. Fisher's wild book, *The Art of Eating*. I suddenly imagined the rain as a twin, each like a hungry being with many mouths, swallowing everything in sight...Of course, I could not resist playing with the aphoristic clichés of 'cats and dogs' who must have also been hungry after all that gust and gale work into the 'future thirst.'"

Katie Chaple lives in Atlanta, Georgia, and is an editor of *Terminus Magazine.* She teaches writing at the University of West Georgia and will serve as the McEver Chair in Poetry this spring in Georgia Tech's program, Poetry@Tech. Her poems have recently appeared in such journals as *32 Poems, The Antioch Review, Bellevue Literary Review, The Chattahoochee Review, Crab Orchard Review, Poet Lore, Southern Humanities Review,* and *Southern Poetry Review.* Her poem "Madame du Barry's Refusal" recently won *Southern Humanities Review's* Theodore Christian Hoepfner Award for poetry.

Chaple writes: "In contemporary American poetry a sub-genre of driving poems exists, and it seems to me that the romance and almost mythic status associated with driving and the open road lends itself quite well to the ode. The very act of driving and the romantic possibilities of new beginnings associated with it are well suited to evoke the acts and purposes of the ode: meditation, love and praise. Whenever poets write, they are always writing odes, whether explicitly or implicitly. The very act of writing implies a kind of love or praise if not for the subject matter or the emotions, events, or objects, then for the world in which they exist."

Maxine Chernoff's most recent publications are *The Turning* (Apogee Press, 2008) and *The Selected Poems of Friedrich Hölderlin* (Omnidawn Press, 2008). She is department chair of the Creative Writing Program at San Francisco State University. She lives in Mill Valley, CA, where she edits *New American Writing.*

Chernoff writes: "'To Soldier' is a poem written as a reaction to the endless war in Iraq, the forces of life and the forces of death."

Kelly Cherry's forthcoming book is *Girl in a Library*, essays about women writers and the writing life. She is the Eudora Welty Professor Emerita of English and Evjue-Bascom Professor Emerita in the Humanities, University of Wisconsin-Madison.

Cherry writes: "I wrote 'Forecast' while I was living in Wisconsin, where the snow, to a native southerner, seemed endless, and only occasionally magical. I was also attuned to Cold War politics, as I had visited what was then the Soviet Union and had friends in Latvia. (My friends and I awaited a day when we could communicate freely.) The snow and the Cold War came together to make 'Forecast.' The poem, of course, is skeptical of storybook endings."

Don Colburn lives in Portland, Oregon, where he is a reporter for *The Oregonian* newspaper. He has published two collections of poetry: *Another Way to Begin*, which won the Finishing Line Press Poetry Prize, and *As If Gravity Were a Theory*, which won the *Cider Press Review* Poetry Award. He has been a finalist for the Pulitzer Prize in feature writing.

Colburn writes: "I'm not sure whether my workshop poem is an ode or not. I do know that it is popular among poets who have attended workshops. I wrote the first draft years ago for an open-mic reading in the now-defunct Back Alley Tavern in Port Townsend, Washington, during a writers' conference. I had just attended a poetry workshop where—trust me—most of the goings-on in the poem never happened. Not exactly, anyway. In a poem, unlike in my day job as a journalist, I get to make things up—or at least make things from. And this poem has acquired a life of its own."

Barbara Crooker's latest collection is *Line Dance* (Word Press, 2008). She has published poems in *The Journal of American Medicine* (JAMA), *Highlights for Children*, *The Christian Science Monitor*, *Denver Quarterly*, *Worlds in their Words: Contemporary American Women Writers* (Prentice Hall), eleven chapbooks, and two full-length books. *Radiance*, her first book, won the 2005 Word Press First Book Award and was a finalist for the 2006 Paterson Poetry Prize. Among her other awards are three Pennsylvania Council on the Arts Fellowships in Literature, the WB Yeats Society of NY Poetry Prize, The Thomas Merton Poetry of the Sacred Award, and the *Rosebud* Ekphrastic Poetry Prize. She lives and writes in rural northeastern Pennsylvania with her husband and adult son, who has autism.

Crooker writes: "I was teaching a workshop and wanted to use a food prompt, so I googled poems about chocolate; when I couldn't find any, I decided to write one myself."

Jim Daniels is the Baker Professor of English at Carnegie Mellon University. His recent books include *In Line for the Exterminator* (Wayne State University Press, 2007), *Revolt of the Crash-Test Dummies* (Eastern Washington University Press, 2007), winner of the Blue Lynx Poetry Prize, and *Mr. Pleasant* (Michigan State University Press, 2007), winner of the Gold Medal for best regional fiction, Independent Publisher Book Awards. He lives in Pittsburgh, PA.

Daniels writes: "In this poem, I was trying to contrast the rude noise of gas-powered lawn mowers with the peaceful grace of the old reel mower. The built-in silences, the fact that you could actually talk to another human being while cutting the grass. I was trying to comment on the sense of community that has been lost in the isolating noise of America. When we run out of grass, maybe the reel mower will make a comeback."

Chad Davidson is an associate professor of literature and creative writing at the University of West Georgia near Atlanta, and author of *Consolation Miracle* (Southern Illinois UP, 2003) and *The Last Predicta* (Southern Illinois UP, 2008). With Gregory Fraser, he also co-authored *Writing Poetry: Creative and Critical Approaches* (Palgrave Macmillan, 2008).

Davidson writes: "I had the memory kicking around in my head of a high school English teacher who once told me that I'd be rich if I found a use for starfish. Since they have the ability to regenerate their appendages, they provide an inexhaustible supply. Though I never found a use for them, I suppose I did accrue some of those riches anyway, at least in a figurative way. What gets regenerated in the poem, however, are the myths surrounding the starfish, the endless chain of signification that surrounds them."

Todd Davis of Bellwood, Pennsylvania, is the author of two books of poems, most recently, *Some Heaven* (Michigan State University Press, 2007). The winner of the Gwendolyn Brooks Poetry Prize, Davis teaches creative writing, environmental studies, and American literature at Penn State University's Altoona College. His poems have been nominated for the Pushcart Prize and have appeared in such journals and magazines as *The North American Review*, *The Christian Science Monitor*, *Indiana Review*, *The Iowa Review*, *The Gettysburg Review*, *5 AM*, *West Branch*, *River Styx*, *Arts & Letters*, *Quarterly West*, *Green Mountains Review*, *Poetry East*, and *Image*. His poems have been featured on the radio by Garrison Keillor on *The Writer's Almanac* and by Marion Roach on *The Naturalist's Datebook*, as well as by Ted Kooser in his syndicated newspaper column "American Life in Poetry."

Davis writes: "'Ode to an Ophthalmologist' literally is an ode to a woman who helped resolve my battle with a chalazion. After months of trying other remedies for the infection, she took me into her surgical theater and sliced me open, scraping me clean. I suppose I had in mind Pablo Neruda's odes, passionate and rhapsodic lyrics to the most ordinary or mundane things. After she absolved me of my infectious sin, I went home immediately and took pen to paper to offer her my thanks. The poem actually hangs in her office to this day."

Carl Dennis lives in Buffalo, New York. His most recent book of poems, *Practical Gods*, his tenth, was published by Penguin in 2007.

Dennis writes: "'On the Bus to Pittsburgh' is intended as a dramatic monologue spoken by an eccentric who is possessed of a vision, like the speaker in Coleridge's 'Ancient Mariner,' though he speaks not to atone for private failure but to reform his failed country."

Travis Wayne Denton lives in Atlanta with his daughter Helena Skylark and is the Associate Director of Poetry@TECH, as well as McEver Chair in Poetry. He also works as an editor of *Terminus Magazine*. His poems have appeared in numerous journals and magazines.

Denton writes: "I believe that a primary goal of poetry is to exalt the world around us—to pull together all the beauty and ugliness and make it into something very concentrated and glorious. The ode takes this goal much further. It amplifies, yet further concentrates—it focuses on the thing itself, whether the thing be a person, an idea, a place. The ode is a way of paying homage to that which we love or hate, that which captivates us. And if the poet does his job effectively, his readers share in that captivation."

David Dominguez's full-length collection of poems, *Work Done Right*, was published by the University of Arizona Press. Most recently, his work appeared in *The Wind Shifts: New Latino Poetry*, University of Arizona Press; *In the Grove: An Homage to Andrés Montoya*; *Bear Flag Republic*, Alcatraz Editions; *Border Senses Literary Magazine*; and *Palabra: A Magazine of Chicano and Literary Art*. He teaches writing and literature at Reedley College.

Dominguez writes: "The first odes that I ever read were by Pablo Neruda; 'Ode to a Dictionary' is my favorite. Neruda wrote those odes for his readers, and so they are public odes, the kind of poems that one might read in Fresno's Fulton Mall not far from Coney Island Hotdog. My ode, however, is introspective and contemplative—a private ode, for it was written during a moment of crisis—a moment in which I wanted to remind myself of that which makes me happy, and, once having rediscovered some of life's essentials, I longed to praise them with the same intensity that I long to eat fresh tortillas."

William Doreski of Peterborough, NH, is the author of *Another Ice Age* (AA Publishers, 2007). His poems have appeared in many journals, including *The Yale Review, The Antioch Review, Harvard Review, Epos, River Styx, Atlanta Review, Notre Dame Review,* and in several collections. He currently teaches writing and literature at Keene State College.

Doreski writes: "This poem concerns itself with the ways in which art and history engage each other in the creation of national and personal narratives. The Hudson River School painters believed that America's natural beauty signaled both God's favor and the glory of our political and social enterprise. Yet to paint this unabashed glory immediately after the horrors of the Civil War, so fresh in the national consciousness, represents an act of will so powerful that if we can accept it we can accede to anything the imagination might inspire—like walking on water."

Denise Duhamel of Hollywood, FL, is the author, most recently, of *Ka-Ching!* (University of Pittsburgh, 2009). She is associate professor of English at Florida International University.

Duhamel writes: "I wrote this poem a few months before I was married, a time when everything around seemed to be bristling with meaning."

Martín Espada was born in Brooklyn, New York in 1957. He has published sixteen books in all as a poet, editor, essayist and translator. His most recent works include *Alabanza: New and Selected Poems* (Norton, 2003) and *The Republic of Poetry* (Norton, 2006), a finalist for the Pulitzer Prize. His awards include an American Book Award and a Guggenheim Fellowship. He teaches in the English Department at the University of Massachusetts-Amherst.

Espada writes: "I write praise-poems in an effort to make the invisible visible."

Richard Fein was a finalist in The 2004 Center for Book Arts Chapbook Competition. He has been published in many web and print journals such as *The Southern Review, Southern Humanities Review, Touchstone, Windsor Review, Maverick, Parnassus Literary Review, Small Pond, Kansas Quarterly, Blue Unicorn, Exquisite Corpse, Terrain* and many others. He also has an interest in digital photography; samples can be found at www.pbase.com/bardofbyte.

Fein writes: "I saw the Trade Center fall while standing on 69th Street in Brooklyn. Many people around me there were extolling Christianity over Islam as if the two were rival political parties. That got me thinking about how religion, all religions, have been misused."

Beth Ann Fennelly of Oxford, MS, is the author of *Unmentionables*, (Norton, 2008). She has published three books of poems and a book of essays, all with Norton. A recipient of a Fulbright to Brazil and grants from the N.E.A. and the United States Artists Foundation, she is associate professor at the University of Mississippi.

Fennelly writes: "This poem lacks many of the traditional qualities of the ode; it's not written in rhyme or regular metrics, it's not of a public nature, and its subject is not dignified (one would be hard pressed to think of anything less dignified than cow tipping). But it does, I think, partake in the rhetorical structure common to the ode—the poet describes an outer scene, meditates on it, and comes to an insight about it."

Carmen Firan, a poet and fiction writer, has published twenty books including poetry, novels, essays and short stories in her native Romania. Since 2000 she has been living in New York. Among her recent books and publications in the United States are *The Second Life*, (Columbia University Press, 2005), *The Farce* (Spuyten Duyvil, 2003), *In the Most Beautiful Life* (poems with photographs by Virginia Joffe, Umbrage Editions, 2002), and three collections of poetry: *New York: Afternoon With An Angel, The First Moment After Death*, and *Accomplished Error*. In 2006, she edited *Born in Utopia: An Anthology of Modern and Contemporary*

Romanian Poetry (Talisman House) with Paul Doru Mugur and Edward Foster. Firan is a member of the Pen American Center and the Poetry Society of America.

Firan writes: "In my adolescence I became intuitively aware of the gravity of words. One night I even got so far as dreaming of them. They were buried at the root of an imposing tree. I was digging with my bare hands, deeper into the guts of the earth, my hands were burning and blood was gushing from beneath my nails, I was pulling weeds, crushing ants and bugs, feverishly searching, perspiring in anticipation, and suddenly, here they were: one by one, perfectly contoured, neat concrete shapes, nothing abstract or incomprehensible about them. Round stones, crystals polished by water, edgy shells, spiral-boned horns, drops of frozen ink, breathtakingly beautiful frescoes, as if torn from a magnificent temple buried at the root of that tree, so that they would be kept hidden, to be uncovered and given to those searching for their essence.

I placed each of them in my palm, carefully cleaned the dirt away and, as I was blowing over them to dissipate the last trace of dust, they became lighter, took airy shapes and flew about me in milky white circles, and then, more and more transparent, they burst like bubbles and disappeared beyond the horizon.

I woke up with a heavy head. Light flooded the room, and instantaneously I forgot everything. But just glancing at my hands, that still hurt, I remembered them digging the dirt at the root of the tree."

Ann Fisher-Wirth lives in Oxford, Mississippi. Her third book of poems, *Carta Marina*, is forthcoming from Wings Press in April 2009. Ann is the author of *Blue Window* and *Five Terraces*, and of two chapbooks: *The Trinket Poems* and *Walking Wu-Wei's Scroll*. With Laura-Gray Street she is editing an international anthology of contemporary ecopoetry in English, *Earth's Body*. She has held Fulbrights to Switzerland and Sweden, and in 2006 she served as President of the Association for the Study of Literature and Environment (ASLE).

Of "Sweetgum Country," she writes: "I teach in the interdisciplinary Honors College at the University of Mississippi. Each spring I ask my freshmen to do a project on environmental issues and present their findings to the class. That the South has suffered, and continues to suffer, appalling environmental damage is everywhere written on the land and in our bodies."

Keith Flynn (www.keithflynn.net) hails from Marshall, NC and is the author of four books of poetry, including *The Lost Sea* and *The Golden Ratio*, and a collection of essays entitled *The Rhythm Method, Razzmatazz and Memory* (Writer's Digest Books, 2007). His poetry and articles have appeared in magazines and anthologies around the world. Flynn is the founder and managing editor of *The Asheville Poetry Review*.

Flynn writes: "Though the ode form is originally attributed to Edmund Spenser and perfected by the Romantics, particularly Shelley and Keats, I like to think of my approach more in the vein of Pablo Neruda whose Elemental Odes in Spanish have had a great impact on many poets and take the Rilkean dictum 'that to praise is the whole thing' strictly to heart when considering their subject matter. 'Virtual Hornets' was written during a Herbie Hancock performance as I watched him slice through fifty years of jazz styles in a single set. It occurred to me that BeBop and Abstract Expressionism as a means of artistic expression had been formed in almost the same era and owed their existence to the same rhythmic forces, hence the allusion to de Kooning and the attempt to paint what a syncopated jazz piece would look like if you could see it."

Diane Gage of San Diego, California, was recently included in *Letters to the World*, a 2008 anthology from Red Hen Press. Gage was born in a very small town on the Montana highline and is also an artist. She belongs to the art group Public Address and teaches a popular poetry workshop for San Diego Book Arts. Poems have appeared in such publications as *Poeisis, Puerto Del Sol, Rattapallax, The Seattle Review, Phoebe, The Chattahoochee Review, Memoir,* and *Hawai'i Review,* among others.

Gage writes: "'Ode To Gravity' is an homage to the great South American poet Pablo Neruda, an attempt to express something of his generous and spacious spirit. South and Central America are America too, a fact North Americans often forget."

Rigoberto González of Queens, NY, is the author of *Men without Bliss* (University of Oklahoma Press, 2008). The recipient of Guggenheim and N.E.A. fellowships, he's a contributing editor for *Poets and Writers Magazine* and on the Board of Directors of the National Book Critics Circle. He's Associate Professor of English at Rutgers University-Newark.

González writes: "My education about the ode comes from Pablo Neruda and Gary Soto—both poets celebrated the everyday things that didn't have to be big to be magical. And since these were personal treasures, they leaned toward the autobiographical and the cultural. In my ode, I chose to focus on this small cartoon icon, which also gave me permission to explore the political."

Kelle Groom lives in New Smyrna Beach, Florida. Her third poetry collection, *Five Kingdoms*, will be published by Anhinga Press in 2009. Groom received a Florida Book Award for her second collection *Luckily* (Anhinga Press, 2006). Her first collection, *Underwater City*, was selected for the University Press of Florida's Contemporary Poetry Series in 2004. Her poems have appeared in *AGNI*, *DoubleTake*, *The Gettysburg Review*, *The New Yorker*, *Ploughshares*, and *Poetry*, among others.

Groom writes: "Neruda's odes in praise of common things—his recognition of the ordinary as fantastic, and Kenneth Koch's moving and playful addresses have long been a great joy for me. More recently, I discovered Barbara Hamby's poem, 'Ode to My Toyota,' in her collection, *Babel*. Her delightful poem inspired mine."

Lola Haskins (www.lolahaskins.com) teaches for the Rainier Writer's Workshop. Her latest poetry collection is *Desire Lines, New and Selected Poems* (BOA, 2004). *Not Feathers Yet: A Beginner's Guide to the Poetic Life* (Backwaters) and *Solutions Beginning with A* (Modernbook)—illustrated fables about women—were published in 2007. Ms. Haskins' awards include two N.E.A.s, the Emily Dickinson Prize from the Poetry Society of America, and the Iowa Poetry Prize.

Haskins writes: "I decided to thank my body for being so patient all these years, so 'Legs' belongs to a series of poems most of which are odes, whether I call them that or not."

Christopher Howell lives in Spokane, Washington, where he teaches in the M.F.A. program at Eastern Washington University's Inland NW Center for Writers, and where he his also senior editor for Eastern Washington University Press. The most recent of his eight books of poems is *Light's Ladder* (University of Washington Press), which won the Washington State Book Award in 2005. Other recent work maybe seen in the pages of *Field*, *The Gettysburg Review*, *Hubbub*, and *The Massachusetts Review*.

Howell writes: "The ode is a lyric poem in praise of a person, place, or thing; though it centers more around the speaker's impulse to praise than around the ostensible subject. Many of the Psalms are essentially odes. The poem 'Gaze' seems to be an ode in praise of memory, until the last few lines when it becomes an ode to the speaker's mother, to her everyday being and the sense of completeness she brought to his life."

Tom Hunley is professor of English at Western Kentucky University, where he serves as director of Steel Toe Books (www.steeltoebooks.com). His poetry has appeared in *TriQuarterly*, *New York Quarterly*, *Los Angeles Review*, and elsewhere, and essays have appeared in *The Writer's Chronicle* and *Review Revue*. His book, *Octopus*, won the third annual Holland Prize from Logan House Press and was published in 2008.

Hunley writes: "My favorite odes are the ones that celebrate the little, quotidian miracles while displaying a child-like sense of wonder: Komunyakaa's 'Ode to a Maggot,' John Olson's 'Ode to a Pizza Tray,' Barbara Hamby's 'Ode to Public Bathrooms,' Ponge's 'The Voice of Things' and Neruda's 'Elemental Odes.'"

James Iredell lives in Atlanta, and is the author of *When I Moved to Nevada* (The Greying Ghost Press, 2008). He was born in Carmel, California, and raised on the central coast. He still makes a drive down the Pacific Coast Highway to Big Sur whenever he visits his family, who (mostly) all still inhabit Northern California. His writing has appeared in *Descant*, *The Literary Review*, *The Chattahoochee Review*, *Zone 3*, and many other places. He's been nominated for the Pushcart Prize, and Best New American Voices. He teaches at Georgia State University.

Iredell writes: "I've worked as a formalist, and as a 'free verse' poet. The odes of Keats and Shelley have always been excellent models of the poet musing on the inexplicable recesses of our minds and souls where art comes from. Maybe, more than anything or anyone, 'Big Sur' is my answer to these guys, with a nod to Frost's *North of Boston,* and Williams' *Paterson.*"

Richard Jackson lives in Chattanooga and teaches at the UT-Chattanooga; he has taught at the Vermont College of Fine Arts, the Prague Summer Programs, Bread Loaf Writers' Conference and Iowa Summer Workshops. He is the author of nine books of poems (most recently *Unauthorized Autobiography: New and Selected Poems* from Ashland Poetry Press), two books of criticism, a book of translations, and winner of Guggenheim, N.E.A., N.E.H., Fulbright and Witter-Bynner Fellowships. He has appeared in five Pushcart, a Best American Poems and other anthologies, and has been translated into fifteen languages. He received the Order of Freedom Award from the president of Slovenia for Humanitarian and literary work.

Jackson writes: "The ode as a form probably began back with the Greeks, especially Pindar, where it had a more formal, triadic and dialectic structure. Later, Horace, in Rome, loosened the surface format but kept the underlying dialectic structure. 'Objects in the Mirror' actually borrows from the Horatian Cleopatra ode (1.39) in its stanzaic structure and overall movement (political-personal-political concerns), and like the ode, is finally intent on a synthesis of the first two terms, here the personal and political. 'Sorrowful Ode' is even looser, more in line with the sort of laments and praises that Neruda or Merwin write."

Robin Leslie Jacobson has taught in programs created by Poets & Writers and California Poets in the Schools. Her training in somatics and the performing arts has deeply influenced her poetry, which has appeared in *Atlanta Review, Poetry East, Bellevue Literary Review, Poetry Flash, Natural Bridge, Runes,* and many other publications. Robin has received honors from American Pen Women, *Ruah* (best chapbook), and Oneiros Press (broadside), and has been a writer-in-residence at the Headlands Center.

Jacobson writes: "The verb 'breathe' represents a healing action for us all, and because I had hip replacement surgery on August 4, to me breathing is healing in a personal sense—bringing oxygen to the place that's undergoing repair. And reading your email today was uplifting, an action that involves not only the mind and spirit but also the body—literally through the mechanism of the breath. To wit, I'm most grateful for the good news at this moment in my life—and for the realizing of your mission at this moment in the life of the planet."

Michael Lee Johnson is from Itasca, Illinois. He lived in Canada during the Vietnam era and is published as a contributor poet in the anthology *Crossing Lines: Poets Who Came to Canada in the Vietnam War Era* published in May 2008. He is also the author of *The Lost American: From Exile to Freedom* (2007). Mr. Johnson has been published in over 19 different countries, and published in 255 different publications worldwide. He is self-employed in advertising.

Johnson writes: "'Tiny Sparrow Feet' is one of many poems I have written from my desk will looking out my balcony window at my huge willow tree and the bird feeder that is between the two. Each day I watch the shrewd behavior of the birds at the feeder, watch the winds in the willow tree, and see the bird devour the golden birdseed."

Janine Joseph was born in the Philippines, and currently lives in Texas where she is pursuing her Ph.D. in Literature & Creative Writing at the University of Houston. Her work has appeared in or is forthcoming from *Third Coast, Spoon River Poetry Review, Nimrod International Journal,* and *Salt Hill.* A Kundiman fellow, she holds a B.A. from UC-Riverside and an M.F.A. from New York University.

Joseph writes: "'Junkyarding through the great Moreno Valley' is one in a sequence of poems celebrating the stalling, clunking, and backfiring vehicles that chauffeured much of her childhood in the ever-sunny, ever-unwalkable Southern California."

George Kalamaras is Professor of English at Indiana University-Purdue University Fort Wayne, where he has taught since 1990. George has published four full-length collections of poetry and three chapbooks, the most recent titles being *The Scathering Sound* (Anchorite Press, 2008) and *Gold Carp Jack Fruit Mirrors* (The Bitter Oleander Press, 2008), as well as poems in many literary journals and anthologies, including *The Best American Poetry 2008* and 1997. He is the recipient of Creative Writing Fellowships from the National Endowment for the Arts (1993) and the Indiana Arts Commission (2001). During 1994, he spent several months in India on an Indo-U.S. Advanced Research Fellowship from the Fulbright Foundation and the Indo-U.S. Subcommission on Education and Culture.

Kalamaras writes: "'As You Breathe in the Slouching' chronicles the first day of several months he spent in India in 1994. He and his wife, Mary Ann, visited the ancient grounds of Lodi Gardens (in Delhi), famous for its Mogul tombs. The paradox of life and death throughout his months in India became a focus for meditation and for this poem—that is, how to hold a series of seeming opposites (including life and death) as complementary rather than contradictory."

Gerry LaFemina is the author of several collections of poetry, including *The Parakeets of Brooklyn* (Bordighera Press, 2004) and *The Window Facing Winter* (New Issues Press, 2004), two collections of prose poems, and a forthcoming collection of short stories. He directs the Frostburg Center for Creative Writing at Frostburg State University, where he also teaches.

LaFemina writes: "I think of an ode as a meditative poem on a particular object (a nightingale) or abstraction (Spring), and as a meditative poet myself, I like that sort of focus. 'Phenomenology of the Vanishing Horizon' was really an ode on distance—on being out of one's landscape, and knowing that by being witness to the phenomena of the natural world in the Caribbean, where the poem takes place. Really it all started with seeing that little shark and thinking, 'Wow. Where's it going?' And that mirrored what I was in the middle of saying about my life."

Peggy Landsman lives in Pompano Beach, Florida. Her first poetry chapbook, *To-wit To-woo*, is available from FootHills Publishing. Peggy Landsman's poetry and prose has been published in both online and print literary journals and anthologies, including *Iodine Poetry Journal,*

Spindle, The Muse Strikes Back (Story Line Press, 1997), *The Largeness the Small Is Capable Of* (Score Press, 2001), and *Bridges* (Indiana University Press). She has a website at http://home.att.net/~palandsman.

Landsman writes: "In 1979, I rewrote Eliot's 'The Love Song of J. Alfred Prufrock.' I called my poem 'The Love Song of a Berkeley Resident.' (I was living in Berkeley, California, at the time.) 'Middle-Aged at the Millennium' comes from the stanza in 'Prufrock' that begins 'No! I am not Prince Hamlet, nor was meant to be...'"

Dorianne Laux lives in Raleigh where she teaches at North Carolina State University. Her most recent book is *Facts about the Moon* (Norton, 2007).

Laux writes: "To sing. Sustained noble sentiment. A dignity of style. And a line from Shakespeare who said: Hangs odes upon hawthorns and elegies on brambles. A hawthorn deserves an ode, a redwood, an elm. Trees sustain me in these dark days fraught with hope. Old trees make me want to sing. I have an ancient red cedar in my backyard in North Carolina. It was there before I was born and will be here after I'm gone. We are all dying every minute. Why not a humble song?"

Carol Lem lives in Sierra Madre, California. Selections of her poems from *Shadow of the Plum*, published by Cedar Hill Publications, can be heard on her CD, *Shadow of the Bamboo*, with music performed and composed by Masakazu Yoshizawa, who is the flute player in "Japanese American National Museum Concert." Other poems by Carol Lem have recently appeared in *The Chrysalis Reader, Blue Arc West,* and *Rattle.* She teaches literature, creative writing, and composition at East Los Angeles College.

Lem writes: "The occasion for this poem was a concert, paying homage to Japanese Americans who were retained at the retention camp in Manzanar. As he plays, the speaker observes people gazing at the photos and memorabilia that belonged to the daughter's father, who taught at the camp. Since the Japanese bamboo flute (shakuhachi), traditionally used for meditation, has five holes, the last line is a comment on that dark period in American history, which the player and speaker/listener are contemplating through the music. 'Japanese American National Museum Concert' first appeared in Writer's at Work ('Sense of Sight' postcard series project)."

Alexander Long's *Vigil* was published in 2006 (New Issues Press). He is co-editor (with Christopher Buckley) of *A Condition of the Spirit: The Life & Work of Larry Levis* (Eastern Washington UP, 2004). His work has appeared in *The Southern Review, Pleiades, Blackbird, Third Coast, Quarterly West,* among others. He is currently an assistant professor of English at John Jay College, C.U.N.Y.

Long writes: "I suppose at least since the world saw photographs and newsreels of the camps in 1945, the ode has become an increasingly challenging—if not downright false—mode of expression for some poets (certainly this one). The ode, then, in this infant century that's already significantly troubled has become for me a kind of prayer borne more by despair than by praise. The ode, then, may have the power to save one (many?) from unequivocal bleakness. Once that happens, perhaps, we can get back to the ode's celebratory origins."

Perie Longo is Poet Laureate of Santa Barbara, has published three volumes of poetry: *Milking the Earth* (1986), *The Privacy of Wind* (1987) and most recently, *With Nothing behind but Sky: A Journey through grief* (2006). Her work has appeared or is forthcoming in *Atlanta Review, California State Poetry Quarterly, Connecticut Review, Eclipse, Nimrod, Paterson Literary Review, Prairie Schooner, Quercus Review, Rattle, Solo,* and *The South Carolina Review.* She is on the staff of the annual Santa Barbara Writers Conference, teaches privately, and with California-Poets-in-the-Schools.

Longo writes: "Some years ago a fourth grade child in one of my California-Poets-in-the-Schools classes wrote on an evaluation of the six week poetry sessions the comment that stuck in my mind 'Every time I write a poem I fall in love with it.' To me, that was the essence of praise, a kind of ode, honoring the joy of writing. This year I was asked to write a love poem for Valentine's day and I remembered the comment which then prompted memories of love-making in the wild with my husband, now deceased, which led to how writing poetry is the one consistent thing that has sustained me through many crises, is akin to making love, has led me from darkness to light."

Alison Luterman's first book of poems, *The Largest Possible Life*, won the Cleveland State University Press Poetry prize and was published in 2001. She also writes essays and plays, including *Saying Kaddish With My Sister* which was produced by the Jewish Ensemble Theatre of West Bloomfield, Michigan in 2008. She teaches creative writing and practices improvisation with the performance ensemble Wing It!

Luterman writes: "I wrote it after a family reunion in Vegas where I watched in fascination as a seventy-year-old peroxide blonde in short-shorts got off a tour bus to go gamble. She seemed so brave and all-American and lonely and determined—she epitomized a lot of what I feel about the West."

Thomas Lux holds the Bourne Chair in Poetry at the Georgia Institute of Technology, where he also directs the McEver Program for Visiting Writers. He is a recipient of three N.E.A. grants, a Guggenheim fellowship, and the prestigious Kingsley Tufts Award. *God Particles*, from where "The Joy-Bringer" comes from, is his eleventh book of poetry. He lives in Atlanta.

Lux says: "The ode gives praise no matter what the subject. 'The Joy-Bringer' is just that: a reason to give praise."

Sebastian Matthews lives with his family in Asheville, North Carolina. His most recent book is *We Generous* (Red Hen Press, 2006). Matthews teaches at Warren Wilson College and serves on faculty for the Low-Residency M.F.A. Program in Creative Writing at Queens University of Charlotte. He co-edits *Rivendell*, a place-based literary journal.

Matthews writes: "I find the ode a perfect early 21st century form. Somewhere between Keats and Neruda, with a little of O'Hara's 'I do, I do that' praise thrown in for good measure. Love for, attention to and wonder at the world we live in, moment by moment."

Derek Mong is the 2008-2010 Axton Poetry Fellow at the University of Louisville. His poems, translations, and prose have appeared in *The Kenyon Review, The Southern Review, Pleiades* and elsewhere. New work can be found in *Crab Orchard Review, The Cincinnati Review,* and *New Delta.* His awards include the Jeffrey E. Smith Prize, a Jay C. and Ruth Halls Poetry Fellowship, and two Pushcartcart nominations. In August he was married on the coast of Oregon.

Of "O h i o" Mong writes: "A friend of mine introducing my work once said 'Derek's poems tonight are brought to you by the letters I and O.' Nowhere is that more apparent than this poem."

Indigo Moore is the author of *Tap-Root* (Main Street Rag, 2006), as well as the recipient of a Cave Canem Poetry fellowship and the 2005 Vesle Fenstermaker Prize for Emerging Artists. Moore is on the editorial board for the *Tule Review* and teaches workshops and residencies at universities throughout the country.

Moore writes: ""Uprooted' is an invocation of the loss of cultural and agrarian identity from a child's viewpoint. The lyric intensity is essential to affecting the emotional core of the poem, maintaining the poem's flow without a stark or harsh element. The slow, uprooting of the stump represents the uprooting of a way of life."

Martin Moran is a graduate of the M.F.A. Program at Colorado State University in Fort Collins, Colorado, where he currently teaches writing and literature. His poems have recently appeared in *Interim, Santa Clara Review,* and *Matter.*

Moran writes: "I came across a book of state flags and their mottos while working as a Park Ranger in Boston Harbor, and was instantly taken by Kansas'—Ad Astra Per Aspera—which translates as 'to the stars through difficulties.' It struck me as emblematic of where we find ourselves as a country, defined by aspiration and struggle yet often lost somewhere between the two. Eventually that phrase became a magnet for all these iconic scraps collected through years of cross country travels, and I suppose the poem took shape as an effort to figure out how these scraps fit together in our present, collective, national context."

Jack Myers, the 2003-4 Texas Poet Laureate, has authored seventeen books of and about poetry, including *Routine Heaven* (Texas Review Press, 2005).   He has taught creative writing since 1975 at Southern Methodist University, where he was its Director of Creative Writing for several years, and in the Vermont College M.F.A. program for 24 years.

Myers writes: "I was thinking back to when I was a kid who, while flirting with danger, felt surely I could be anything I wanted; and how that stood directly opposite to my feeling as an adult, who's been burned a lot by the mistakes in judgment I've made, that one's choices become more and more limited as one becomes older and better defined; and how these diametrically opposed feelings exist within the American Dream which is nestled inside a tacit corporate plutocracy."

Kate Northrop's first collection, *Back Through Interruption* (Kent State University, 2002), received the Stan and Tom Wick Poetry Award and was runner-up for the Great Lakes New Writers Award. Her second collection, *Things Are Disappearing Here* (Persea Books, 2007), was the finalist for the James Laughlin award and an Editor's Choice for *The New York Times Book Review*. She is currently an associate professor of English/ Creative Writing at the University of Wyoming and Contributing Editor at *The American Poetry Review*.

Northrop writes about "Night Skiers": "Although I had severed a tendon in my right hand and therefore couldn't ski, I accompanied a friend on a ski trip to Jackson Hole, Wyoming in the winter of 1994. I spent most of my time in the public library, which I remember as being at the base of the mountain, or close enough anyway that, at twilight, I could watch the last of skiers coming down. They were beautiful and silent and strange; I tried for a month or so to write a poem about those moments, then I gave up, then I (maybe) succeeded suddenly in the middle of the winter of 2005 when I was heart-broken, and yet, it turns out, hopeful."

She writes: "'The Pure Beauties' came to me whole, drawn into existence by the repeating phrase, referring to the pure beauties, 'there they go.' I can no longer remember when I wrote the poem but it feels autumnal, inspired perhaps by teaching at the college level. The students (I am old enough now) seem terribly beautiful, because they are young when they appear, and they are still young when they leave. As I was aware that the poem risked sentimentality, I was pleased to discover that image, 'alone as a small child,' which added, I hope, an edge to the poem."

Naomi Shihab Nye is the author of *You and Yours* (BOA Editions, 2005), which received the Isabella Gardner Poetry Award, *19 Varieties of Gazelle: Poems of the Middle East* (HarperTeen, 2002), *Fuel* (BOA Editions, 1998), and others. She has been a Lannan Fellow, a Guggenheim Fellow, and a Witter Bynner Fellow. She lives in San Antonio, TX.

She writes: "I fell in love with Pablo Neruda's exquisite odes to—socks, etc.—many years ago. It has always seemed that the presence-of-mind needed to focus on anything and write about it as well as the detailed affection which odes require, is very helpful for daily life."

Elise Paschen's next poetry collection, *Bestiary*, will be published by Red Hen Press in spring 2009. Elise Paschen is the author of *Infidelities*, winner of the Nicholas Roerich Poetry Prize, and *Houses: Coasts*. Her poems have been published in *The New Republic*, *Ploughshares* and *TriQuarterly* among other magazines, and in numerous anthologies, including *A Formal Feeling Comes* and *The POETRY Anthology, 1912–2002*. Editor of *The New York Times* best-selling anthology *Poetry Speaks to Children* and co-editor of *Poetry Speaks Expanded* and *Poetry in Motion*, Paschen teaches in the Writing Program at The School of the Art Institute of Chicago.

Paschen writes: "After visiting Fort Zachary Taylor, Key West, in January 2003, the image of the armament buried beneath the sand haunted me, and I began writing 'Sanctuary,' revising the poem over these past years. I adopted the triptych structure during those first drafts and later realized the poem was a contemporary ode in that an ode traditionally divides into three movements. The poem's subject matter, the desire for safety under threatening circumstances, reflects the public concerns of the ode, and I consider 'Sanctuary' an anti-war poem."

Alison Pelegrin is the author of *Big Muddy River of Stars*, winner of the Akron Poetry Prize; as well as *The Zydeco Tablets*; and three prize-winning chapbooks, most recently *Voodoo Lips* and *Squeezers*. Individual poems have appeared in *Poetry*, *Ploughshares*, *The Southern Review*, *Shenandoah*,

Poetry Daily and *The Writer's Almanac.* She earned an M.F.A. from the University of Arkansas, and is the recipient of an Individual Artist Fellowship from the Louisiana Division of the Arts. Presently teaching English at Southeastern Louisiana University, she lives in Mandeville, Louisiana with her husband, Bryan Davidson, and their two young sons, Ben and Sam.

Pelegrin writes: "The poem began as a catch-list to give to these contractors we hired to fix our house after Katrina, only they left town before the work was finished. This happened a few times, though I don't know what I expected. The way I hired people was by chasing official-looking pickup trucks down the street until they stopped, and asking them what they were good at. We moved in our house before it was truly repaired, and I remember writing this poem at the kitchen table—no curtains in the now mismatched bay windows, while our last crew of workers patched things up."

Stanley Plumly's work has been honored with the Delmore Schwartz Memorial Award and nominations for the National Book Critics Circle Award, the William Carlos Williams Award, and the Academy of American Poets' Lenore Marshall Poetry Prize. He has received a John Simon Guggenheim Memorial Foundation Fellowship, National Endowment for the Arts Awards, Pushcart Prizes, an Ingram-Merrill Foundation Award, and an Academy Award in Literature from the American Academy of Arts and Letters. Plumly's recent books include *Now That My Father Lies Down Beside Me: New and Selected Poems, 1970-2000* and *Old Heart.* He has taught at many universities around the country, including the Universities of Iowa, Michigan, and Washington; Ohio University; Princeton; Columbia; the University of Houston; and New York University. He is currently a Distinguished University Professor and Professor of English at the University of Maryland.

On "Still Missing the Jays" Plumly says: "I was alarmed some years ago when I suddenly realized I hadn't seen a blue jay in years. It turns out that someone in the local government where I live [in Maryland] had decided that crows were a nuisance, and set out to poison them. Blue jays and magpies are first cousins to the crow, and it seems they—along with numerous other birds—suffered the same fate as the crows. This piece is actually a companion piece to 'Missing the Jays,' both poems which appear in my latest collection *Old Heart*. Some five years after writing, 'Missing the Jays,' I finally saw a small one, inspiring this companion piece."

Dawn Potter is associate director of the Frost Place Conference on Poetry and Teaching. Her most recent books are a memoir, *Tracing Paradise: Two Years in Harmony with John Milton* (University of Massachusetts Press, 2009), and a poetry collection, *How the Crimes Happened* (CavanKerry Press, 2010). New poems and essays appear in *The Sewanee Review, The Threepenny Review, Prairie Schooner,* and elsewhere. Her poems, essays, and reviews have appeared in journals such as *The Journal, Ninth Letter, Coconut, Court Green, Memorious,* and *The Georgia Review*. She earned her Ph.D. at the University of Georgia, and now earns her keep as a copyeditor for university presses. She lives in Davis, California.

Potter writes: "This ode began as an homage to Pablo Neruda, and those who also love his odes will recognize its debts. I wrote these eclogues after spending time with Virgil's eclogues; and I realized, as I was reading them, how much his poems foreshadow the personal odes of the Romantic poets, with their passionate descriptions of the natural world and their link between the outer life and an inner human dilemma. Yet as I was writing my eclogues, I found myself wanting to break away from the steady stanza structures of Shelley and Keats. Because I frequently write in traditional forms, I can only guess that my poems' fractured narrations of the age-old pains of love required a similar uneven form."

Dorine Preston is a Ph.D. candidate in English at the University of Georgia, where she has been the Assistant to the Editors of *The Georgia Review*. A Seattle-area native, she earned her M.F.A. in poetry from New Mexico State University. Her poems and reviews have appeared in publications such as *Puerto Del Sol, Verse, Isotope, New Delta Review, Court Green, Coconut,* and *Ninth Letter*. She is a winner of a 2005 Dorothy Sargent Rosenberg Memorial Poetry Prize, and receieved an honorable mention in the 2005 *Atlantic Monthly* Student Writing Contest..

Preston writes: "This ode began as an homage to Pablo Neruda, and those who also love his odes will recognize its debts."

Bill Rasmovic's poems most recently appeared in *Gulf Coast* and *Caffeine Destiny*. His first book, *The World in Place of Itself*, was published by Alice James Books in 2006. He is a pharmacist in Manhattan and has acted as literary excursion leader and workshop co-leader with Richard Jackson of UT-Chattanooga throughout Switzerland, Italy, Croatia, Slovenia, Germany and Wales.

Rasmovicz writes: "The ode in this case was simply nod to/ an acknowledgement to the former lives had, especially the ones hardly remembered. Invariably, they've shaped us."

William Reichard is the author of three collections of poetry, including *How To* (Mid-List Press, 2004) and *This Brightness* (Mid-List Press, 2007). His new collection of work, *Sin Eater*, will be published in 2010. He teaches seminars on writing, art, and social justice for the Higher Education Consortium for Urban Affairs.

Reichard writes: "This poem was written in honor of my friend, Clara (Kitty) Couch. Kitty, a ceramic artist, was one of the few self-actualized people I've ever met. Though she passed on a few years ago, her presence and patient knowledge continues to have a profound impact on my life as an artist."

Jack Ridl of Holland, Michigan, has just retired from 37 years of teaching at Hope College. He has published three chapbooks and three full collections including *Broken Symmetry* (Wayne State University Press, 2006) and *Against Elegies* (The Center for Book Arts/NYC Chapbook Award.) A new collection, *Losing Season*, will be published in 2009 by CavanKerry Press.

Ridl writes: "When writing this poem, I was thinking of the meditative nature of the English ode and how this man, with two weeks to live, might consider writing within such a tradition. By writing only the last lines of poems, in one sense he is able to give his 'last words' to the world while leaving all that leads up to those last lines to remain in his and our minds. I guess that it's an ode without an ode, an ode-less ode. Or perhaps this ode is closer to a particular truth of his life, the one that lies beyond articulation."

Karen Rigby resides in Gilbert, Arizona. Her second chapbook, *Savage Machinery*, was published by Finishing Line Press in 2008. Poems have appeared or are forthcoming in *Black Warrior Review*, *Line Break* and other journals. She writes mostly lyric poems and can be found at www.karenrigby.com.

Rigby prefers to let her ode speak for itself.

Alberto Ríos has taught at Arizona State University for over 26 years, and is currently a Regents' Professor and holds the Katharine C. Turner Distinguished Chair. He is the author of nine books of poetry, three chapbooks, three short story collections, and a memoir. His *The Smallest Muscle in the Human Body* (Copper Canyon Press, 2002) was a finalist for the National Book Award.

Ríos writes: "This poem was written at the request of Arizona's governor to contextualize the visit of President Vicente Fox of Mexico, on his visit to Arizona several years ago. I read the poem for the first time in front of several thousand people, including the governor and the president, and let the words of the poem challenge the sensibilities of the visit, suggesting that we have a choice of viewing the border as either the place the separates us or the place that joins us. The challenge is simple, but profound. When I spoke to the president afterward, he said that he liked the words of the poem. I said that, yes, I liked the words, too, but that the actual job of the best of those words was yet to be realized. We both laughed and he nodded his head once more in a sadder but determined yes. I grew up in Nogales, right on the border with Mexico, born of immigrant parents from Mexico and England. We lived the border, joyously. I can't find or recognize that border anymore, though I keep looking."

William Pitt Root, a former Teamster, bouncer, PITS poet, writer-in-residence at Amherst, Interlochen, and NYU, has seen his writing translated into twenty languages. He has also held Guggenheim, Stegner, N.E.A., Rockefeller and US/UK fellowships. While Tucson's Poet laureate, he commuted to NYC weekly to teach at Hunter College.

The New York Times calls his poems "marvelous ...rangy, virile, startling for their sophistication, pungency and force." His current book is *White Boots: New & Selected Poems of the West* (Carolina Wren Press, 2006).

Root writes: "I was living in an old adobe house with a leaky tin roof on 20 wild acres outside Oracle, Arizona, translating some of Neruda's early *Odas Elementales*. The exuberance of the improvisational energy and free form (tall, skinny, suited for newspaper columns) were contagious. I had to try one. Glancing around... aha! That tall glass of water chilling a bouquet of celery stalks. I'd quit smoking, an annual ritual then. The writing was such fun I didn't even think about cigarettes. Until I finished. It's hard to keep celery lit."

Sankar Roy, originally from India, is a poet, translator, activist and multimedia artist living near Pittsburgh, PA. He is a winner of PEN USA Emerging Voices, author of three chapbooks of poetry—*Moon Country, The House My Father Could Not Build* and *Mantra of the Born-free* (all from Pudding House). He is an associate editor of the international poetry anthology, *Only the Sea Keeps: Poetry of the Tsunami* (Rupa Publication, India and Bayeux Arts, Canada). His poems have appeared or forthcoming in over sixty literary journals including *The Bitter Oleander, Crab Orchard Review, Connecticut Review, Harpur Palate, Tampa Review, Runes, Rhino* and *Poetry*.

Roy writes: "An Ode is a celebration and elation of the heart! 'Ode to America' was composed in this poet's mind while passing through an American boulevard in the twilight of night."

C. J. Sage resides in Rio Del Mar, California, where she works as a Realtor. She also edits *The National Poetry Review* and teaches poetry at De Anza college. Her poems appear in *Ploughshares, Shenandoah, The Antioch Review, The Threepenny Review, Prairie Schooner, Black Warrior Review, POOL, Backwards City Review,* and other venues. Sage's books are *Odyssea, Field Notes in Contemporary Literature, And We the Creatures,* and *Let's Not Sleep.* She may also be a bit goat-like.

Sage prefers to have her ode speak for itself.

Dixie Salazar has published three books of poetry: *Hotel Fresno* by Blue Moon Press in 1988, *Reincarnation of the Commonplace* (national poetry award winner) by Salmon Run Press in 1999, and *Blood Mysteries* by University of Arizona in 2003. *Limbo*, her novel, was published by White Pine Press in 1995. She has also published numerous poems and some short stories in about sixty different literary journals, including, *The Missouri Review*, *The Red Brick Review*, *Poetry International* and *Ploughshares*, as well as anthologies such as *Many Californias*, *Unsettling America* and *Highway 99*. Currently she teaches English at California State University and shows oil paintings and collage work at the Silva/ Salazar studios at 654 Van Ness in Fresno, California. She has also taught extensively in the California prisons and the Fresno County jail.

Salazar writes: "The poem 'Altar Where I Watch You Sleep' is part of a series of altar poems, which I see as secret odes. An altar of course is a celebration of various elements that spark off each other, and I see that as part of how the poetic process works. And in this poem, once again, I am enchanted by and inspired by the sea. Radcliffe Squires, an old professor of mine, expansively, inclusively, defined the ode as 'a serious poem on a serious subject,' that is, an attitude more than a form. Note, 'serious' does not mean morose or humorless, but rather earnest at heart and substantial in subject. Whether public or private, formal or free, an ode wrestles with big issues."

Adrian Sângeorzan lives in New York City. He is the author of several books of poetry and fiction: *Over the Life Line*, 2002; *Voices on the Razor's Edge*, 2003; *Between Two Worlds—Tales of a Women's Doctor*, 2003 (second edition, 2004); *Tattoos on Marble*, 2006; *The Circus in Front of the House*, 2007 (second edition 2008). His works are part of several anthologies published in France, Germany, UK, Romania, and the US.

Sângeorzan writes: "I grew up and got most of my education in communist Romania. I imagined myself retiring somewhere up in the Carpathian Mountains, somewhere far from all that political craziness. After I immigrated to the States I contemplated my retiring in Florida, where I felt like owning a piece of sand which seems to be at the same time far and close to everything."

John Savoie's poems have appeared in *Poetry, Natural Bridge* and *Shenandoah,* and his first collection, *Metaphysical,* is ready for a publisher. He teaches Great Books at Southern Illinois University-Edwardsville.

Savoie writes: "My poem, 'Summer Is Here,' responds to the ethnic conflicts that bedeviled Serbia and Kosovo in 1999, especially from the perspective of the American midwest (so the relatively peaceful "lee") where many emigrants from that violence have settled. Sadly, ten years later, the poem retains a topical relevance."

Vivian Shipley is the Connecticut State University Distinguished Professor and the Editor of *Connecticut Review* from Southern Connecticut State University and has published five chapbooks and seven books of poems. In 2007, she was inducted into the University of Kentucky Distinguished Alumni Hall of Fame, won the Hackney Literary Award for Poetry from Birmingham-Southern University in Alabama and the New Millennium Poetry Prize. A new book of poetry, *All of Your Messages Have Been Erased,* is forthcoming in 2009 from Southeastern Louisiana University Press in Hammond, Louisiana.

Shipley writes: "Evil will not be tamed, widespread injustice will not be curbed. I wrote this poem as an ode to bear witness to the thirty two who were killed at Virginia Tech whose bodies ensnared by a power that cannot be understood or controlled were strewn about like debris after a suicide bombing. While Seung-Hui Cho's random act of violence was inexplicable, it was not random because violence is deeply embedded in our culture."

Jane Shore is the author of four books of poems: *Eye Level,* which won the 1977 Juniper Prize; *The Minute Hand,* which won the 1986 Lamont Prize; *Music Minus One,* which was a finalist for the 1996 National Book Critic Circle Award; and *Happy Family* (1999.) She is a professor at The George Washington University and lives in Washington, DC and in Vermont.

Shore writes: "I grew up in an apartment above my family's dress store in New Jersey, and clothing (literally and metaphorically) is a recurring image in my poems. I think that clothes have presences and personalities, and that old clothes can haunt you—the bad luck dress you were wearing when you received the phone call that your father died—the good luck outfit you had on when you got your first kiss. Are you wearing the clothes or are the clothes wearing you?

When my own daughter was growing up, I was amused to see her evolve through different stages of dressing up. When she became a teenager I was shocked to discover that the clothes that she wanted looked exactly like the clothes that I myself had worn (and disposed of) thirty years before.

And so, like many poets before me, I hoped to downplay the idea of the ode as an heroic, elevated poem of praise, and personalize and recycle it, just like the 'vintage' clothes that always seem to come back into style."

Barry Silesky lives across the street from Wrigley Field in the heart of Chicago, where for more than twenty-five years he has witnessed the repeated fire and extinction of America in the century's fate of the Cubs, which of course spills into all his poems. His fourth collection, *This Disease*, came out last year ('07) from Tampa Review Press, to go with biographies of Lawrence Ferlinghetti (Warner Books) and John Gardner (Algonquin Press). He taught for many years at The School of the Art Institute of Chicago, where "The New Treaty" originated, in the work of another faculty.

Silesky prefers to let his ode speak for itself.

Warren Slesinger was a university press editor for several years. He now teaches at the University of South Carolina-Beaufort. His poems have been published in several literary magazines.

Slesinger writes: "On a cross-country trip, I discovered, sadly, what 'agri-business' has done to the landscape and the small farmer."

Arthur Smith lives in Knoxville, Tennessee. His most recent book of poems is *The Late World* (Carnegie Mellon, 2002). Earlier books are *Elegy on Independence Day* (University of Pittsburgh Press, 1985), and *Orders of Affection* (Carnegie Mellon, 1996). Recent poems have appeared in *The Georgia Review, Poems & Plays, Atlanta Review, Hunger Mountain,*

Poetry International, and *TriQuarterly.* He is Professor of English at UT-Knoxville.

Smith writes: "I hesitated when I was asked to write an ode celebrating the bicentennial of the founding of the University of Tennessee. I had been teaching the possibilities of the ode and saw this as an opening to subordinate the classical form to the content of the contemporary world. And so I jumped. If classically the human and divine worlds were juxtaposed, now the comparisons would be not between the human and the divine, but between one set of experiences with another set, as one way of understanding."

Gerald Stern lives in Lambertville, NJ. His two most recent books are *Everything is Burning* (2005) and *Save the Last Dance* (2008), both from Norton.

Stern writes: "'Last Blue,' which was written in 1998 or 1999, is a study of blue in all its aspects, sad and happy, and connects 'blue' with the very center of existence and of the poet's existence. It is, for me, a critical, a basic poem."

Maria Terrone of Jackson Heights, NY (www.mariaterrone.com), is the author of *A Secret Room in Fall* (Ashland Poetry Press, 2006), co-winner of the McGovern Prize. Other poetry collections include *The Bodies We Were Loaned* (The Word Works, 2002) and *American Gothic, Take 2,* a chapbook (forthcoming spring 2009, Finishing Line Press). Poems have appeared in *Poetry, The Hudson Review, Notre Dame Review, Atlanta Review* and many national anthologies. Terrone is assistant vice president for communications at Queens College, City University of New York.

Terrone writes: "The literary concept for 'A Fruited Plain,' a lyric inspired by a nearby market, came to me on a crowded subway platform at my home station in Queens. But it was at my brother's kitchen table in Vermont—far from my familiar, multi-ethnic environment—that I composed this work. Phrases from 'America the Beautiful' woven throughout are intended to resonate with new, more complex meaning in our post-9/11 world in this poem that celebrates my neighbors—dream-seekers and strivers from every corner of the globe."

Pamela Uschuk's "Healing in the Language of Trees" was published in *Scattered Risks* (Wings Press, 2005), which was nominated for a Zacharias Prize by *Ploughshares*. The poem is the subject of an independent film being made by prize-winning California independent filmmaker, Lucinda Luvaas. Uschuk teaches at Fort Lewis College in Durango, Colorado.

Uschuk writes: "I wrote this poem after recovering from a ruptured spinal disc that immobilized me for six weeks. Almost daily, I underwent intensive physical therapy and had to lie flat on my back. Doing nothing physical was excruciating. I remember watching trees that fall, the way their leaves danced wildly in wind. They were the antidote to my immobility, to the war, car bombs and destruction in Iraq and the Middle East."

Wendy Vardaman of Madison, WI, has a Ph.D. in English from the University of Pennsylvania. A collection of poems, *Obstructed View*, is forthcoming from Fireweed Press in 2009. Her poems, reviews, and interviews have appeared in a variety of anthologies and journals, including *Riffing on Strings*, *Letters to the World*, *Poet Lore*, *Poemeleon*, *qarrtsiluni*, *Main Street Rag*, *Nerve Cowboy*, *Free Verse*, *Wisconsin People & Ideas*, *Women's Review of Books*, *Rain Taxi Review*, and *Portland Review*. She home schools two of her three children and works for The Young Shakespeare Players.

Vardaman writes: "'St. Catherine of Siena's Day' employs some traditional elements of odes, such as a tripartite structure, and alludes to odes by English Romantic poets, although its subject matter, the relation of domesticity to spirituality and to aesthetics, is less obviously elevated, and the poem's irregularly metered couplets are meant to suggest that tension. Both daffodils and dandelions are in season in Madison on St. Catherine's feast day, April 29th."

Jon Veinberg lives and works in Fresno, CA. He is the author of four poetry collections and has been published in numerous anthologies and literary magazines. His latest collection is *The Speed Limits of Clouds* (C&R Press, 2009). He has been a two-time recipient of an N.E.A. grant.

Veinberg writes: "In 'Preaching for Winos' the speaker, the preacher troubadour of blighted street corners, is singing praises to any wino audience that will listen. And through his song he is honoring his own lived through experiences and in an ability to exalt and exploit change, both individually and subliminally, hoping to stretch his listeners toward salvation."

Benjamin Vogt is a Ph.D. candidate in poetry and creative nonfiction at the University of Nebraska-Lincoln. His work has appeared in *Crab Orchard Review, Diagram, Hayden's Ferry Review, Puerto del Sol, Verse Daily*, and a chapbook, *Indelible Marks* (Pudding House). His writing has been nominated for a Pushcart Prize and received several awards, including a grant from the Dorothy Sargent Rosenberg Memorial Fund.

Benjamin sees the ode "as a way to connect people to place, and vice versa. In 'Japanese Garden,' a prose poem formed by individual haiku, different components of the garden design contribute to a larger whole. Through looking at a meaningful place in this way, the garden and the gardener become the same voice, the same subject, the same being—an ode to one another."

Diane Wakoski lives in East Lansing, MI, and continues to teach as a University Distinguished Professor at Michigan State University. She has published more than twenty collections of poetry, the most recent being *The Butcher's Apron* (Black Sparrow Press, 2000).

Wakoski writes: "The ode, a poem of address, essentializes intimate speech as private mediation."

Suellen Wedmore, Poet Laureate emerita for the small seaside town of Rockport, Massachusetts, has been published in *College English, Green Mountains Review, Atlanta Review* and many others. A first-place-winner in the *Writers' Digest* Rhyming Poem Contest, she recently was selected for a Writer's Residency at Devil's Tower, Wyoming, and her chapbook *Deployed* won first place in the Grayson Books annual contest.

Wedmore writes: "In addition to being entertained and inspired, I was moved by the poignancy of Pablo Neruda's odes to common things, as in 'Ode to an Artichoke,' 'Ode to the Onion,' and 'Ode to my Socks.' It is the small things, of course, that make up the texture of our lives. And the repository of the everyday to a child of the 50s and 60s was Woolworth's! What fun I had writing this poem—going into my past to try to express the importance of the trivial represented by this American institution."

Gary Young's books include *Hands, The Dream of a Moral Life*, winner of the James D. Phelan Award, *Days, Braver Deeds*, winner of the Peregrine Smith Poetry Prize, and *No Other Life*, which won the William Carlos Williams Award of the Poetry Society of America. His most recent books are *Pleasure*, and *Bear Flag Republic: Prose Poems and Poetics from California*. His *New and Selected Poems* is forthcoming from White Pine Press. He has received a Pushcart Prize, a fellowship from the National Endowment for the Humanities, and two fellowships from the National Endowment for the Arts. He edits the *Greenhouse Review Press*, and his print work is represented in many collections including the Museum of Modern Art and the Getty Center for the Arts. He teaches at the University of California-Santa Cruz.

Young writes: "We spend each moment as an integer in a complex design. The value of any particular instant is, of course, past all calculation."

Permissions and Acknowledgments

We are grateful to the authors who have given us permission to include previously unpublished work in this anthology. We also thank the authors, editors, and publishers who have given us permission to reprint poems at little or no charge, asking only to be acknowledged. As a 501(c)3 press, we value the production and support of good writing above all else.

Kim Addonizio, "God Ode" will appear in her forthcoming collection, *Lucifer at Starlite* (Norton) and is printed with permission of the author.

Dick Allen, "Quiet" was published in a previous collection by Sarabande books and by permission of the author.

Ralph Angel, "Part I: Acknowledgment" from *Exceptions and Melancholies: Poems 1986- 2006*, Sarabande Books, Louisville, KY, 2006.

James Arthur, "In Defense of the Semicolon" first appeared in *Brick* (2003) and is reprinted with permission of the author.

Sally Ashton, "Remembered Lines on Way to Stockton" will appear in her forthcoming collection, *Don't Look Down*, and is printed by permission of the author.

David Baker, "To Winter" and "Midwest Ode" are reprinted from *Changeable Thunder* (University of Arkansas Press, © 2001 by David Baker) and appear with permission of the author.

Barry Ballard, "Ode to Red Riding Hood" appears by permission of the author.

Robin Behn, "Elegy: Cook County" appears by permission of the author.

Marvin Bell, "The Book of the Dead Man (His Olde Ode)" published by *The Gettysburg Review*, copyright © Marvin Bell 2008.

Eleanor Berry, "Ode in Shades of Green" appears by permission of the author.

Erin M. Bertram, "My Tattoo" first appeared in *CutBank*, and again in *A Sing Economy* (Flim Forum Press, 2008) as part of the sequence 'Bestiary with a Broken Window & a Thin Though Not Unkind Smattering of Light' and appears by permission of the author.

Michelle Bitting, "Endurance" appears in *Good Friday Kiss*. Reprinted by permission of C&R Press.

Craig Blais, "Ode to Memory: Self-Portrait with Seven Fingers II" appears by permission of the author.

Bruce Bond, "North: 1991" appears by permission of the author.

Laure-Anne Bosselaar, "English Flavors" copyright © 1997 by Laure-Anne Bosselaar. Reprinted from *The Hour Between Dog and Wolf*, by Laure-Anne Bosselaar, with the permission of BOA Editions, Ltd.

Earl Sherman Braggs, "Miles Davis Plays Trumpet at the Funeral of Malcolm X" appears in *In Which Language Do I Keep Silent: New and Selected Poems*, and by permission of the author.

Sean Brendan-Brown, "A Night So Pure the Love of God Seemed Real," first appeared in the Winter/Spring 2004 issue of the *Birmingham Poetry Review* and appears by

Bliss (University of Oklahoma Press, 2008), and is reprinted by permission of the author.

Kelle Groom, "Ode to My Toyota" first appeared in *Poetry* and appears by permission of the author.

Lola Haskins, "Ode to My Legs" was first published in *The Georgia Review* and appears by permission of the author.

Christopher Howell, "Gaze" originally appeared in *Field*. The poem is also the title piece of a book forthcoming next year from Milkweed Editions. It appears by permission of the author.

Tom Hunley, "Awe to Ennui" first appeared in *Birmingham Poetry Review #27*, Summer/Fall 2003, and is reprinted by permission of the author.

James Iredell, "North of Big Sur" appears by permission of the author.

Richard Jackson, "Sorrowful Ode" first appeared in *Prairie Schooner* and "Objects in this Mirror" first appeared in *Unauthorized Autobiography: New and Selected Poems* (Ashland Poetry Press). Each are used by permission of the author.

Robin Leslie Jacobson, "A Summer without Ice" appears by permission of the author.

Michael Johnson, "Tiny Sparrow Feet" appears by permission of the author.

Janine Joseph, "Junkyarding through the Great Moreno Valley" first appeared in *Bear Flag Republic: Prose Poems and Poetics from California* (Greenhouse Review Press, 2008) and appears by permission of the author.

George Kalamaras, "As You Breathe in the Slouching" first appeared in *The Marlboro Review*, is reprinted from Kalamaras's book *Gold Carp Jack Fruit Mirrors* (The Bitter Oleander Press, 2008). It appears by permission of the author.

Gerry LaFemina, "Phenomenology of the Vanishing Horizon" appears by permission of the author.

Peggy Landsman, "Middle-Aged at the Millennium" appears by permission of the author.

Dorianne Laux, "Trees" appears by permission of the author.

Carol Lem, "Japanese American National Museum Concert" first appeared in the "Writers At Work" postcard series, and appears by permission of the author.

Alexander Long, "Ode to Bombs" first appeared in *Askew* and then in his first collection of poems, *Vigil* (New Issues 2006). It is reprinted by permission of the author.

Perie Longo, "What We Live For" will be published in the 2008 California-Poets-in-the-Schools Statewide Anthology, and is printed by permission of the author.

Alison Luterman, "Ode to Vegas" is printed by permission of the author.

Thomas Lux, "The Joy-Bringer" first appeared in *American Poetry Review*, and is included in *God Particles*. It appears by permission of the author.

Sebastian Matthews, "Skywalker," and "Morning Lines with Horses Running Through" appear by permission of the author.

Derek Mong, "O h i o" first appeared in *Alehouse 2* (winter 2007) #49 where it won the 2007 Happy Hour Poetry Award and appears by permission of the author.

Martin Moran, "America" appears by permission of the author.

Indigo Moor, "Uprooted" was first published in *Tap-Root* (Main Street Rag, 2006), and appears by permission of the author.

Jack Myers, "Duds" originally appeared in *Langdon Review of the Arts in Texas*, Vol. 4,

2008 (Tarleton State University, Granbury, TX) and appears by permission of the author.

Naomi Shihab Nye, "Muscat Sundown" appears by permission of the author.

Katherine Northrop, "Night Skiers," and "The Pure Beauties" first appeared in *Raritan* and *Sewanee Theological Review*, respectively. They were also collected in her second collection, *Things Are Disappearing Here* (Persea Books, 2007). They appear by permission of the author.

Elise Paschen, "Sanctuary" will appear in her next collection of poems, *Bestiary* (Red Hen, 2009), and is printed by permission of the author.

Alison Pelegrin, "Ode to Contractors Possessing Various Levels of Expertise" appears by permission of the author.

Stanley Plumly, "Still Missing the Jays" first appeared in *Blackbird*, and was reprinted in *Old Heart* (Norton, 2007) and appears by permission of the author.

Dawn Potter, "Eclogue I": *Off the Coast* (January 2006); "Eclogue II":*Blue Collar Review* (summer 2005); "Eclogues III and IV": *Interpoezia*, no. 2. All four eclogues appear in *How the Crimes Happened* (CavanKerry Press, 2010) and appear by permission of the author.

Dorine Preston, "Ode to Doubt" first appeared in issue 9 of *Memorious* and is reprinted by permission of the author.

Bill Rasmovicz, "Ode to a Childhood Photograph" appears by permission of the author.

William Reichard, "Clara's Vision" appears by permission of the author.

Jack Ridl, "During the Last Two Weeks of His Life, He Wrote Only the Last Lines of Poems" was originally published in this form in *Prairie Schooner*. Re-published in *Broken Symmetry* (Wayne State University Press) and appears by permission of the author.

Karen Rigby, "Ellis Island" appears by permission of the author.

Alberto Ríos, "Border Lines" first appeared in *Virginia Quarterly Review* and is reprinted by permission of the author.

William Pitt Root, "Under the Influence of Celery" first appeared in *Many Mountains Moving* (1997) then in *Fever Dreams: Contemporary Arizona Poetry*, ed. L. Wright and J. Cervantes (University of Arizona Press, 1997), and is reprinted by permission of the author.

Sankar Roy, "Ode to America" appears by permission of the author.

C.J. Sage, "Goat" appears by permission of the author.

Dixie Salazar, "Altar Where I Watch You Sleep" appears by permission of the author.

Adrian Sângeorzan, "Florida" first appeared in his collection *Tattoos on Marble* and appears by permission of the author.

John Savoie, "Summer is Here" appears by permission of the author.

Vivian Shipley, "An Ode to Virginia Tech, Blacksburg, April 16, 2007" appears by permission of the author.

Jane Shore "Shopping Urban" first appeared in *A Yes-or-No Answer* (HoughtonMifflin, 2008) and appears by permission of the author.

Barry Silesky, "The New Treaty" appears by permission of the author.

Warren Slesinger, "Wheat" appears by permission of the author.

Arthur Smith, "Late Century Ode for the Common Dead" first appeared in *Crab*

Orchard Review (1,1, Fall/Winter 1995) and is reprinted by permission of the author.

Gerald Stern, "Last Blue" first appeared in *Last Blue* (Norton, 1998) and appears with permission of the author.

Maria Terrone, "The Fruited Plain" appears by permission of the author.

Pam Uschuk, "Healing in the Language of Trees" was first published in *Scattered Risks* (Wings Press, 2005). The poem appears by permission of the author.

Wendy Vardaman, "St. Catherine of Siena's Day" appears by permission of the author.

Jon Veinberg, "Preaching for Winos" appears in *Highway 99, Homage to Vallejo* and in his forthcoming collection, *The Speed Limit of Clouds* (C&R Press, 2009). The poem appears by permission of the author.

Benjamin Vogt, "Japanese Garden" appears by permission of the author.

Diane Wakoski, "Ode to My Hands" is reprinted from *Poetry Southeast*, Summer 2006 issue and appears by permission of *Southeast Review* and the author.

Suellen Wedmore, "Ode to the Five and Dime" appears by permission of the author.

Gary Young, "*the earth submits to seasonal drift*" is from *In the Face of It: New and Selected Poems* (White Pine Press, 2010) and appears by permission of the author.

Subject Index

Nature

"Small" Subjects

Title Index